Juanita's Gift

A Saints Book Written by a Sinner

Russell F Morrison

Copyright © 2014 by Russell F Morrison
All rights reserved.

ISBN: 1500320102
ISBN 13: 9781500320102
Library of Congress Control Number: 2014911667
CreateSpace Independent Publishing Platform
North Charleston, South Carolina
Scripture quotations marked NIV are taken from the Holy Bible, New International Version®. NIV®. Copyright © 1973, 1978, 1984 by International Bible Society. Used by permission of Zondervan Publishing House. All rights reserved.

Scripture quotations marked KJV are taken from the Holy Bible, King James Version.

Scripture quotations marked NKJV are taken from the New King James Version®. Copyright © 1982 by Thomas Nelson, Inc. Used by permission. All rights reserved.
He Changed His Last Name- by Mary May Larmoyeux. Copyright © 2014 by FamilyLife. All rights reserved Used with permission

Scripture quotations marked WEB are taken from the World English Bible, which is based on the American Standard Version, first published in 1901. Public Domain.
Scripture quotations marked ESV are taken from the English Standard Version.

Acknowledgments

Robin Berry - Photograph for book cover
David Nelson - Walking with God through Lymphoma and Beyond

Brenda Burton – Christ Like
Wanda Hitt - Randy's Story
Denise Gale - God's Perfect Timing
Coby Smith - Tasso

Sara and David Rhodes - Grandma's story
Patti Morrison - Michelle's Story
Liz and Kenny Hill - God's Couch
Sheron Wiess -God's Couch
Raymond Whitten - A Rock in the Caribbean
Liz Bray - Amber's Story
Rob Hernandez - He Changed His Name
*Chellie and Dale Longstreth - But As For Me and My House,
We Will Serve The LORD.*

Becky Parker - Son Died God Restored His Life

Linda Callahan- Linda's Story
Jerry Sprout - Jerry's Story
Charlee Morrison - Children Who Pray
Lillian Morrison - Children Who Pray
Katheryn Bannon - Reading Glasses
Jewell Crowson- Can a Boat be an answer to My Prayer?

Juanita's Gift

A Saints Book Written by a Sinner

To my three grandchildren

Charlee, Lillian, and James

Contents

Chapter 1 Seven Steps to Answered Prayer 1
Chapter 2 Trusting God 9
Chapter 3 Walking with God through Lymphoma and Beyond 17
Chapter 4 Are You Willing to Pay the Price? 27
Chapter 5 Christ Like 31
Chapter 6 The Camping Trip that Changed My Life 37
Chapter 7 Confession Brings Life. 43
Chapter 8 Walking In the Spirit 49
Chapter 9 Obedience 55
Chapter 10 Intercessory Prayer. 61
Chapter 11 We Have the Right to Use the Name of Jesus. 67
Chapter 12 God's Reason for Creation 71
Chapter 13 The Holy Spirit. 83
Chapter 14 Vacation to Israel 89
Chapter 15 Get in Position to Receive 105
Chapter 16 Amber's Story 111
Chapter 17 Fervent in Prayer. 119
Chapter 18 No Poverty in Christ. 123
Chapter 19 There Are No Valleys in Jesus 127
Chapter 20 Healing. 131
Chapter 21 Wavering Faith 139
Chapter 22 Linda's Story. 143
Chapter 23 Be Perfect in God. 147
Chapter 24 He Changed His Last Name 153

Chapter 25 Fruit of the Spirit 157
Chapter 26 Enemies of Love 163
Chapter 27 Juanita's Daily Prayers 167
Chapter 28 Peace of God 179
Chapter 29 Tasso 185
Chapter 30 Jesus Gives Us Peace 191
Chapter 31 Randy 197
Chapter 32 How to Be Perfect in Your Love Walk 203
Chapter 33 Perfecting Our Love Walk 209
Chapter 34 God's Perfect Timing 215
Chapter 35 A Vessel Fit for the Master's Use 219
Chapter 36 Pleasing God 223
Chapter 37 Children 231
Chapter 38 Charlee's Faith 237
Chapter 39 Faith 245
Chapter 40 Fruit of Our Lips 251
Chapter 41 Greater Health God's Way 257
Chapter 42 Eleven Ways You Can Get Rid of Stress 263
Chapter 43 My Near-Death Experience 271
Chapter 44 Building the Temple 279
Chapter 45 Life and Power of Words 283
Chapter 46 Renewing Your Mind 289
Chapter 47 Spiritual Authority 293
Chapter 48 A Rock in the Caribbean 297
Chapter 49 Renew Our Relationship 305
Chapter 50 Children Who Pray 309

Foreword

I'm very pleased to be able to unwrap another gift of my mother-in-law's daily journals and share them by putting them into this book.

Our parents and, in many cases, mentors leave us something behind when they leave this earth. They leave us with their ideas of life and their knowledge of what is right or wrong and which path in life we should take. I was left with a little bit more than that. I was blessed with her journals, which were filled full of wonderful jewels of faith and hope that can carry us throughout this life.

This spiritual giant left her family and friends an example of the gifts that she embraced daily. By embracing the gifts of the spirit she took on the same reflection of Christ. Those attributes that she adopted into her daily walk caused her to be able to share her kindness to others in need. She had the patience to listen when those around her were hurting and the ability to trust in her faith, even when the odds were impossible to overcome.

My mother-in-law left three decades of her journals, recording her personal study of God's Word and the drive to search for truth. Once I read these journals, I was so inspired to share her personal study that I put them into a book. I believe that she continues to share her faith with others through this book.

Preface

Juanita Rinehart was a lady who eagerly strived to walk as close as she could with her personal Savior. This desire was so strong that it motivated her to do her best in everything she pursued in life. She was at the top of her class in high school and college. Although she and her sister, Johnnie Cox, and brother, Jack Haynes, were from the humble town of Clarksville, Arkansas, they shared a mutual passion for embracing almost any challenge in life and usually coming out on top.

Even among the three siblings, there was an underlying competitiveness that encouraged them to greater achievements in almost everything they did. As the youngest of the trio, Jack affectionately made sure both his sisters knew that he had finished a little above them in college. This friendly rivalry would continue through their lives as they aimed high and lived life to the fullest.

Johnnie became a school teacher, and Jack became a pharmacist. Juanita became a school teacher but later joined her husband in working at her brother's drug store in Benton, Arkansas.

Juanita longed to be a good wife and a loving mother and, more than anything else, to enjoy a close walk with God. She was fond of saying that she wanted to be "on the first flight to heaven" when the rapture occurred or whenever the Lord decided to take her home. She victoriously embraced that option when the Lord called her home in 2008.

As her son-in-law, I was blessed to receive the wonderful gift of her daily journals, which she wrote during a lifetime of meditation on God's Word. Once I began reading her journals, I was amazed by the wealth of wisdom the Lord had revealed in and through her. I knew in my heart that I needed to share the fruits of her lifework with others. Juanita's journals are a treasure trove of insight into a life of faith and spiritual sustenance. Her notes and prayers have changed my life, and I hope they will do the same for you. It's my prayer that this collection of journals will inspire others to study and dig for deeper meaning in their own walk with God.

My mother-in-law took time each day to journal about her study of God's Word so she could share with others about her faith. She was always very generous with her time and money and took time out each day to pray for others throughout her life.

This book is about a spiritual woman who never gave up on her belief in God and wanted others to have the same opportunity at a life filled with peace, joy, and hope for a life after this one. She kept detailed notes so that she could recall special services that she attended throughout her life. The gift of her notes was given to me, and I will continue to share them with as many people as I can.

Juanita left her family one amazing thing, her personal notes and journals. These journals continue to enlighten all of us on what type of Christian she was. Reading all of her journals kept me wondering why she kept such an extensive collection of notes. I really think she wanted

Preface

her family to read and share them. It was her passion for life that she left behind, that is, she left us a gift.

This book will give you the insight of her faith and how she trusted God for everything in her walk. For those that take time to read and study what she left behind, it is all about one thing: her love of God and sharing the message of her faith.

The journals were full of her ideas about her prayer life, obedience, and how the first man had fallen from grace and caused all of mankind to be born into sin. She wanted to share with everyone that we have a way out of this darkness by finding the light of Christ and becoming a new creature in Christ by accepting the good news of Christ. Her hope was for us to believe in His word.

I have added a few stories of faith along the way to share how she changed my life and the lives of her children and grandchildren.

One niece who lives in the state of Washington thought Juanita was a little out there with her faith and later realized how cool she really was after reading the first book I compiled, Juanita's Walk with God.

After reading the first book several of Juanita's nieces were sharing the book with all of their friends. You know Juanita must have been jumping for joy in heaven to have her book in the hands of all her loved ones. I'm not talking about just one of the nieces—several of them were sharing her book with others.

This Scripture in 1 Timothy really caused me to think about how I rate my own walk with God. Paul noted that he was the chief of all sinners.

"This is a faithful saying, and worthy of all acceptation, that Christ Jesus came into the world to save sinners, of whom I am chief."

(1 Timothy 1:15 KJV)

That's how I feel when I try to compare myself with my mother-in-law's walk with Jesus. I will continue to keep challenging myself each and every day, and by faith I will be able to walk a little closer to him. We all need to be challenged to do better each day. I know the only way is through prayer, study, and keeping my mind on Him and the Word.

During many years of being her son-in-law, I watched every step she took and couldn't help but notice she wanted to stay on the same path that Jesus walked. I can say she walked in His spirit and His love. I have never in my life been so inspired to do something like putting her wonderful notes and study journals into a book. God can take a piece of raw rough clay and mold it into whatever He wants. I feel that God is molding me every day by taking her study of God's Word and building her notes into a book that I feel is inspired by God.

Juanita was such a humble person who gave her all to Christ. She was always trying to achieve perfection in His Spirit. Like Paul in the Bible, she wanted to walk daily toward perfection in His walk: "Let us therefore, as many as be perfect, be thus minded." We need to have the mind of Christ.

I had a lot of fun naming this second book Juanita's Gift: A Saint's Book Written by a Sinner. For the many decades that I knew Juanita, I thought she pretty much walked on water when it came to her study of the Word and her prayer life with Jesus. I know it must be hard to believe something like this, coming from a son-in-law, but it is the truth.

Preface

During my life I have not seen many individuals rise as early as she did in the morning to start her pray communion with God and then go to work. I have felt much honored to be able to put together another book together from her many journals, and I want to share them with as many people as I can. When watching her for many decades I realize that I have a long way to go with my own walk, but I feel I am getting closer each day to walking in the Spirit as she did.

Paul wrote, "I'm the chief of all sinners." I hope one day I can have the same prayer life and strong unchallenged faith that Paul and Juanita did. I still feel I have a long-distance run before me, and I need to stand up like Paul did and proclaim what is mine. I will keep pressing toward the mark of the high calling and walk as Jesus walked toward the light of God's love.

> *"When Jesus heard it, he saith unto them, 'They that are whole have no need of the physician, but they that are sick: I came not to call the righteous, but sinners to repentance.'"*
>
> (Mark 2:17 KJV)

The good news is that no matter how serious the sin, God is always seeking us out and is willing to forgive and forget our sins and give us a fresh start. As long as we are alive, it is never too late to ask for forgiveness and make a fresh new start. You can become a new creature in Christ just by asking.

Reading Juanita's journals has been such a wonderful gift to our family and our small community of Benton, Arkansas, and has helped my wife and me overcome some very difficult times that have tried to trip us up. Reading them has brought peace back into our daily lives.

What is a gift?

> *A gift or a present is the transfer of something without the expectation of payment. Although gift-giving might involve an expectation of reciprocity, a gift is meant to be free…By extension the term gift can refer to anything that makes the other happier or less sad, especially as a favor, including forgiveness and kindness.* (Wikipedia)

There are a few things I want to make clear before you read Juanita's Gift a Saints book written by a sinner, plus how the book is laid out. I thought my mother in law was an exceptional person of faith and I would call her a saint for living the way she did. When I compare my daily walk as a Christian I would say I'm the sinner who put her great notes into this book.

I found that her personal study had become a wonderful gift of instructions to help me strive to have the spiritual walk that I can be proud of. By applying a few of her basic principles of praise, prayer and faith, I feel that I'm heading in the right direction.

Even though I feel we are all born into sin I think most of us know we have a ways to go before we are Christ like. The first step to become a true believer is to have a child like faith and accept Him by faith. Juanita was the same way, in her writings she examined herself daily and wanted to make sure she followed God's will in her personal walk so she could be ready to walk into His presence at any time.

There are several parts that make up the book. Juanita's personal journals that are full of her study of the Bible. All scriptures quotes and my comments will be in italics throughout the book. I have written a few stories along the way and several other stories were given to me by my

Preface

close friends who were inspired to share their stories of faith throughout the book as well.

I will continue to share this wonderful gift of her journals with as many people who take the time to read them.

INTRODUCTION

Where Are the Women of Faith?

This book will give you the insight that you need in order to know where women of faith are and what they are doing. They always seem to be supporting every aspect of our world that we live in, by supporting their family's friends and co-workers. They keep us going in the right direction, which is toward the light of the Most High God.

This book is a study of the Bible that comes from a woman of faith who wanted to share her Christian thoughts to the small town of Benton, Arkansas. She would wake up around 5:00 a.m. to study and meditate on God's Word. She would take detailed notes while she studied and read for hours, even before her family ever thought of getting out of bed.

When her family did pull themselves out of their warm beds that she had made, it was time for breakfast and then time to help her son prepare for school. (Her daughter had moved out of her mother's home and had been married for nine years by the time she was preparing these notes.) Then, it was off to work with her husband, who was very demanding of her time.

She started out as a school teacher and then later became a pharmacy tech so that she could help her brother and husband at their family-owned drug store. She would be the hands and feet of her husband so that his work load would not be too demanding. She pretty much ran most of the day and then it was time to return home and start working again while the family rested. It was during this same very full routine that she would study for hours each day. In addition she taught Bible studies for teenagers, young adults, and the seniors at her church.

I have taken her notes for the second time, the notes that she made so that she could share her faith on the radio and to anyone who would listen in this book. I have also included a few heartwarming stories from my friends and family throughout the book to add to the very uplifting and positive journal notes that Juanita noted each day of her life.

I think she is one of the many women in our society who have cared for their children, community, and country. They always seem to be in the background, making sure we are going in the right direction and that our paths are clear of any obstructions. They are always ready to take care of any issues that seem to get in their family's way that might prevent them from achieving the goals they have set for them. God loved this woman and kept her while she lived this demanding life until her death in 2008.

In her writings Juanita was at first "meeting with" herself, but later she began to share with a larger audience whenever she had the opportunity. She would go out into the community to share with others how many ways we can serve the Lord, e.g., by praying, by studying the Word of God, and by walking as Jesus did by faith.

She would share with others how, in the beginning, the first man Adam caused all of mankind to fall into darkness. She shared with us throughout her studies that there is a spiritual darkness and that without God there is nothing but darkness. She wrote that the world knows the Word of God and that once you have accepted Him, He becomes our Father.

My mother-in-law was not shy about telling you about her faith. These notes were prepared by her so she could share her faith with as many people who would listen, as she spoke on her local radio station and in the Bible studies that she was giving.

I hope her notes speak to your heart as much as they have to mine. I have found out there are a lot of great women out there who have made a huge impact on their families—and even sons-in-law—in a positive way.

I have been very blessed to have had a mother that I loved dearly and who through much opposition took me to church and tried her best to make sure I had a Christian upbringing. She was a wonderful person who loved her family but had many struggles and limitations of her own to slow her down in this life. She had a wonderful wit and that great sense of humor that kept me and her going. She had such a contagious laugh that it could make everyone in the room laugh.

My dad was a very hard worker who had demons in his life that he could never seem to overcome. I loved them both and am so glad I have been born into a world in which there are no limitations for people like me and my sister due to our faith in God, which helped us through difficult times as children. We made it through those times and Christ carried us through those trying days so that we could share our faith and hope with others who have had a tough childhood and the struggles in life that never seem to stop coming.

I give thanks for my mother who never gave up on me. She left this earth when she was only fifty-two years old, and my dad passed away at sixty-four. They both had very challenged lives full of diversity that kept coming at them until it took both their lives at an early age. I was so blessed to have my wife and her family to keep me going even though, at times, I was not a positive person. I had many people who came into my life to help change that.

Here are Juanita's Rinehart's notes that have challenged me to study God's Word each and every day.

Chapter 1

Seven Steps to Answered Prayer

1. Decide what you want from God and get the Scripture that definitely promises you those things. Be definite and specific with God. If you need healing, find a Scripture and pray that.

   "He himself bore our sins" in his body on the cross, so that we might die to sins and live for righteousness; "by his wounds you have been healed."
   (1 Peter 2:24 NIV)

2. Meditate on the Word. Study it until you find the Scripture. Then pray it—believe it. Wait on the Lord; fight the fight of faith. Stand on the Word you've prayed. Tell the Devil, "It is written," and then quote him the Scripture.

   Juanita would say, "In the Name of Jesus, Devil, you don't have any authority to do anything in my family's life or mine. Now get out!" And she meant it.

3. Ask God for the things you want, and believe that you have them. God knows what we need, but He wants us to ask for His help.

"Ask and it will be given to you; seek and you will find; knock and the door will be opened to you. For everyone who asks receives; the one who seeks finds; and to the one who knocks, the door will be opened."

(Matthew 7:7-8 NIV)

"Therefore I tell you, whatever you ask for in prayer, believe that you have received it, and it will be yours."

(Mark 11:24 NIV)

"Praise be to the God and Father of our Lord Jesus Christ, who has blessed us in the heavenly realms with every spiritual blessing in Christ."

(Ephesians 1:3 NIV)

Everything we need has been provided for us from Jesus. We can't see them, but they are there. That which is in the spiritual realm is made real in the natural realm through my faith. My faith grasps it and creates the reality of it in my life. When you pray, believe that you have them and you shall receive them. We are not walking in sense knowledge or by sight, but we are walking by faith. Believe that you receive. How do we act when we receive something joyous? We'll be joyous and happy.

4. Let every thought and desire affirm that you have what you ask. Never permit a mental picture of failure to remain in your mind. Never doubt for one minute that you have the answer. Our faith creates reality. We are to stand our ground and refuse to be defeated. Acting on God's Word brings results. Keep a mental picture of what you've prayed for.

Thoughts are governed by observation, association, and teaching. Stay away from all places and things that do not support your affirmation that God has answered your prayer.

"Finally, brothers and sisters, whatever is true, whatever is noble, whatever is right, whatever is pure, whatever is lovely, whatever is admirable—if anything is excellent or praiseworthy—think about such things. Whatever you have learned or received or heard from me, or seen in me—put it into practice. And the God of peace will be with you."
(Philippians 4:8, 9 NIV)

The Bible tells us what to think and meditate on. Many people are focusing on the wrong things and they get tripped up.

The Word says, "Throwing down imaginations and every high thing that is exalted against the knowledge of God, and bringing every thought into captivity to the obedience of Christ." When you pray God's Word, don't let the devil put negative thoughts into your mind. It is so easy to let things of this life control you.

5. Meditate constantly on the promises (from God's Word) upon which you based the answer to your prayer. See yourself in possession of what you've asked for. Make plans accordingly as if it were already a reality.

"My son, attend to my words. Turn your ear to my sayings. Let them not depart from your eyes. Keep them in the center of your heart. For they are life to those who find them, and health to their whole body."
(Proverbs 4:20, 21, 22 NIV)

God will make His Word good to us if we act on it. God's Word says, "He Himself took our infirmities and bare our sicknesses, and by His stripes we are healed." If after you have prayed this Word for healing you don't see yourself well, then God's Word has departed from your eyes. Remember God only works and moves in line with His Word. God is bound by His Word. He stands behind His word to perform it.

"If you remain in me, and my words remain in you, you will ask whatever you desire, and it will be done for you."

(John 15:7 WEB)

6. See yourself in the reality of what you have prayed. If you have prayed for healing, see yourself well, not sick. If you have prayed for a financial need, begin to see that need met.

   In your waking moments, think on the greatness of God and His goodness, and count your blessings and your faith will increase. Lift your heart constantly in praise for what God is doing and what He has done.

   "Do not be anxious about anything, but in every situation, by prayer and petition, with thanksgiving, present your requests to God."

   (Philippians 4:6 NIV)

   God does not want us to be anxious in anything. Take time in your day to trust in Him, and the worries of the day will no longer be affecting you.

7. Make every prayer relative to what you've asked as a statement of faith instead of unbelief. This means thinking faith thoughts

and speaking faith words that lead the heart out of defeat and into victory.

Do not accept "no" as an answer, and do not be denied. It is your family right, your redemption right, your gospel right, and your creative right to have what God has promised for us. It will come and it is ours now, so accept it and it will become a reality. Many times we undo our prayers. We will pray and, instead of thanking God, we continue to pray the same thing over and over. Well, we are praying unbelief. God has said it; I believe it; that settles it.

1. Pray God's Word.
2. Believe you receive what you pray.
3. Meditate on God's Word, and the answer to your prayer will come.

If you ever asked Juanita to pray for you, you better get ready for a prayer that would turn your world around.

Can a Boat be an answer to My Prayer?

Jewell Crowson's story

One story that I heard just in the last few months was about a young couple who just adored Juanita and her strong faith. They asked her to pray with them about their urgent need for a few dollars to help them make the next month's rent and pay some bills.

The man, who is a few years older now, told me that Juanita didn't just say she would pray for them "later." She would say, "Let's pray right now in the name of Jesus that the needs will be met and the money you need for your family would be coming in, and that Jesus would take care of your needs."

A few days went by and the man won a boat. A coworker called him and said, "I would like to look at the boat and make you an offer to buy it." Wow! The boat was sold, and the needed money came in like clockwork. That was one of many prayers that were answered when Juanita prayed.

Many of her longtime friends would ask her to pray for just about anything that was going on in their lives. It could be for a health issue or finances or finding a job. She would not let that person who asked for prayer walk away without her saying, "Let's believe. Where two are gathered and believe, your prayers will be answered in the Name of Jesus."

God's Couch

Liz and Kenny Hill, a young couple with two very rambunctious boys, were in need of a new couch. Because they are firm believers in not only the Lord, but also in practicing good stewardship regarding finances, they were not able to go and purchase one from the local furniture store. They decided they would pray about their need and trust in God to provide.

They were very specific in their needs for their new couch and together came up with the list. Sturdy enough to stand up to the boys, comfortable for Friday Night Family Movie time, durable covering, (leather) and could not cost more than $175.00.

They sat down together to pray and thank God for the many blessing they had been given. They asked God for the couch with the specifics listed above. Their neighbor, Mr. Bernie, came over on his way to church that morning and asked Kenny if he knew of anyone who needed a new couch. You see, his son had purchased new furniture for his office and was selling leather, La-Z-Boy couch for only $175.00

The couch is affectionately referred to as "God's Couch" because He knew the need of this family and answered a prayer.

Chapter 2

Trusting God

Trust—confide in and rely on—be confident in what you believe, knowing that what He says will come to pass. Throw yourselves completely and totally into the arms of God.

> *"Do not be afraid, little flock, for your Father has been pleased to give you the kingdom. Sell your possessions and give to the poor. Provide purses for yourselves that will not wear out, a treasure in heaven that will never fail, where no thief comes near and no moth destroys. For where your treasure is, there your heart will be also."*
>
> (Luke: 12:32–34 NIV)

Our Father tells us not to fear. He wants us to believe and be confident in Him. There is no fear in walking in Christ. Fear comes from Satan.

> *"For the Spirit God gave us does not make us timid, but gives us power, love and self-discipline."*
>
> (2 Timothy 7 NIV)

For God didn't give us a spirit of fear, but of power, love, and self-control.

We are not given the spirit of fear. Just trust God in everything you do.

Fear comes in to rob us of our faith. Trusting Him comes from the study of the Word of God.

"What if I'm not healed?" God continues to be in control of all things, so don't fear.

There was a very sick woman who thought if she could only touch a small piece of Jesus' clothes she would be healed just by her faith.

> *"Then he said to her, "Daughter, your faith has healed you. Go in peace."*
> *While Jesus was still speaking, someone came from the house of Jairus, the synagogue leader. "Your daughter is dead," he said. "Don't bother the teacher anymore."*
> *Hearing this, Jesus said to Jairus, "Don't be afraid; just believe, and she will be healed."*
>
> (Luke 8:48-50 NIV)

God says, Fear not, flock. Trust in Me.

For most of us, stepping out in faith and trusting in God can be very hard. Our society wants us to trust in things that we can taste, touch, and see and not things that don't seem to be a reality. So one thing I'm going to do is step out in faith and trust in those things that I can't see, which the spiritual realm is. One thing you can do: Rely on Jesus.

> *"When the disciples saw him walking on the lake, they were terrified.*
> *"It's a ghost," they said, and cried out in fear.*
> *But Jesus immediately said to them: "Take courage! It is I; don't be afraid."*

> *"Lord, if it's you," Peter replied, "tell me to come to you on the water."*
>
> *"Come," he said.*
>
> *Then Peter got down out of the boat, walked on the water and came toward Jesus. But when he saw the wind, he was afraid and, beginning to sink, cried out, "Lord, save me!"*
>
> *Immediately Jesus reached out his hand and caught him. "You of little faith," he said, "why did you doubt?"*
>
> (Matthew 14:26–31 NIV)

As long as Peter looked at Jesus with his faith eyes he did not sink. The instant Peter started thinking about what was going on doubt came in. Fear gripped every part of his being until the hand of Jesus pulled him up.

Don't let your mind take you down the road of doubt when Jesus is right there by your side each and every day. He really is walking with us through good times and bad. Just trust in Him.

One thing to remember during these very uncertain times is a comment that Jesus said during His ministry: Fear Not. Placing your trust in Him will ease the pain that so often comes into our world.

> *"And he directed the people to sit down on the grass. Taking the five loaves and the two fish and looking up to heaven, he gave thanks and broke the loaves. Then he gave them to the disciples, and the disciples gave them to the people. They all ate and were satisfied, and the disciples picked up twelve basketfuls of broken pieces that were left over. The number of those who ate was about five thousand men, besides women and children."*
>
> (Matthew 14:19-21 NIV)

When we get our eyes off Jesus, we get over into a realm of the natural, a realm where fear can come in.

It is the same way with us as with Peter: the minute we get our eyes off of Jesus—out of the faith realm—fear grips us and we go down. Jesus said, "Why did you doubt?"

> "Therefore don't be afraid of them, for there is nothing covered that will not be revealed. So do not be afraid of them, for there is nothing concealed that will not be disclosed, or hidden that will not be made known. What I tell you in the dark, speak in the daylight; what is whispered in your ear, proclaim from the roofs. Do not be afraid of those who kill the body but cannot kill the soul. Rather, be afraid of the One who can destroy both soul and body in hell. Are not two sparrows sold for a penny? Yet not one of them will fall to the ground outside your Father's care. And even the very hairs of your head are all numbered. So don't be afraid; you are worth more than many sparrows."
>
> (Matthew 10:26-31 NIV)

Jesus was saying to as many who would listen, "Fear them not. We trust in God—He is with us. The Holy Spirit is in us. The evil in the world can't do anything against us."

> "But the angel said to her, "Do not be afraid, Mary; you have found favor with God."
>
> (Luke 1:30 NIV)

Mary found favor with God because she was submissive to His will. God has chosen all of us to take part in His wonderful plan. One thing we must do is align ourselves with His Word and take time out of each day to open our hearts to His spiritual guidance.

> "Good will come to those who are generous and lend freely,
> who conduct their affairs with justice.

Surely the righteous will never be shaken;
they will be remembered forever.
They will have no fear of bad news;
their hearts are steadfast, trusting in the Lord.
Their hearts are secure, they will have no fear;
in the end they will look in triumph on their foes."

(Psalm 112:5–8 NIV)

When our hearts are established and fixed on God, we can truly put our trust in God and know for certain we can rely on every word that God has promised in the Holy Scriptures. *No matter what anyone says or does, no matter what circumstance comes into your world, just continue to be fixed on God. Trust Him, and do not allow anxious thoughts to come in to control your walk. Trust in your faith and keep meditating on His Word.*

"In God I trust and am not afraid.
What can man do to me?"

(Psalm 56:11 NIV)

When it was time for Juanita to walk into the presence of God in 2008, she would repeat how she loved Jesus and praised God. She repeated those words until she was gone. What a testimony of her faith, that even in death she was going to trust in Him.

"Cast your burden on God, and he will sustain you. He will never allow the righteous to be moved."

(Psalm 55:11)-KJV)

Every day of our lives we need to just lay our burdens on Him and believe that He can overcome whatever is troubling us.

> "Trust in the Lord with all your heart and lean not on your own understanding;
>> in all your ways submit to him, and he will make your paths straight."
>>> (Proverbs 3:5–6 NIV)

Juanita wrote that we should never get over into the thought realm, running it around in our minds. "Shuck it on the Lord." *I loved it when she wrote "shuck it on the Lord." You can tell that Juanita was from the "Deep South."*

One thing I do know: life can be very stressful. Once I place my trust in God, it causes me to have a day at peace. You know, every time I let my mind wander, I seem to lose control. I get anxious and let my mind run away with thoughts that take me down a road I don't need to go down. Just stay focused on God, and trust, Him that all things will work out for you. I love the words to this song: "If it doesn't kill you, it will make you stronger." I saw a clip on the Internet of a young woman who was fighting cancer. She and her nurses were lip-syncing, "If it doesn't kill you, it will make you stronger." She was so right. What a positive attitude to have. She was not going to let cancer beat her. Our daughter Charlee was the same way. She never gave up. And with that positive attitude, it helped her stay alive on this old earth for eight more years. I believe God wants us to trust in Him and never give up. Regardless of the outcome, we will meet Him on the other side.

> "You will keep in perfect peace those whose minds are steadfast, because they trust in you."
>> (Isaiah 26:3 NIV)

> "But blessed is the one who trusts in the LORD, whose confidence is in him.
>> They will be like a tree planted by the water that sends out its roots by the stream. It does not fear when heat comes; its leaves are always green.

It has no worries in a year of drought and never fails to bear fruit."

The heart is deceitful above all things and beyond cure. Who can understand it?

"I the Lord *search the heart and examine the mind, to reward each person according to their conduct, according to what their deeds deserve."*
(Jeremiah 17:7–10 NIV)

Will we be like a tree planted by the water, rich and full of life? He that trusts God has entered into His rest.

Chapter 3

Walking with God through Lymphoma and Beyond

"My Story" by David Nelson

As a young man, I was very lost—but I was a seeker. So much so, in fact, that the mother of a girl I once delighted in wrote a whole page of encouragement to me in the opening flap of a Bible that she pressed into my hands when I departed for a planned year of studying in Japan. Pointing me toward my Creator, she cautioned me on the dangers of being a seeker in a land where Christians are rare. "I will pray for you often," she promised, and pray for me she did.

After seven years of exploring a spiritual wilderness in Japan, my canteen was running over with exotic adventures in the practice of Buddhism, Shinto, Zen rituals, Hare Krishna chants and home gatherings, channeling sessions with disembodied spirits, and all manner of New Age philosophies. The philosophical exploration was a rich experience, perhaps, intellectually, but a lack of moral compass and the spiritual hangovers from New Age indulgences opened my eyes to an ever-intensifying sense of hopelessness and frustration. Although I was beginning to realize that I was a sinner, I was spiraling ever downward. I didn't understand it yet, but I was desperately hungry for the truth and redemption that only a Savior could offer.

In God's perfect timing, He introduced me to a sweet Japanese woman who would later become my wife. I met Yuko in an Aikido martial arts class, of all places, but it didn't take me long to discover that she was fond of reading the Bible. This grabbed my attention and began drawing me closer to the Savior I so desperately wanted to meet. After searching so long for a Truth that evaded me, I realized that the Bible was one horizon I had never fully explored.

In time, we married and began to "play church." I had grown up in a rather watered-down church, biblically speaking, so I assumed that I was a Christian after all. Then I met a couple of fellows who invited me into a Bible study. I learned that I had never given my life to Christ, but I also learned that my knowledge of Scripture was dangerously shallow. The group was part of a dangerous "Christian cult" that almost trapped me into following their "Salvation-by-Works" model, but the Lord used my wife to introduce me to Christian counselors who helped me out of that trap. The one best thing the Lord allowed me to learn from the cult experience was that people really can be excited about studying Scripture, and, *yes*, there really can be churches where people are genuinely passionate about their faith. I accepted Jesus Christ as my Savior, and He brought other believers into our lives who introduced us to a solid Bible church where we began to grow in our faith. I had no idea then what a terrible time of testing the Lord was preparing us for.

A few years later, in 1997, after twelve years in Japan as a photojournalist, I went home to visit my family in Little Rock and was diagnosed with non-Hodgkin's lymphoma, stage four—the most advanced stage that usually points to impending mortality. Just a year earlier, I had been a very healthy and fit young man of thirty-six, when my first child, a little fellow named Sean, was born. A PET scan revealed that the disease had spread throughout most of my body, especially in the bones. Further diagnostics revealed that I might have hope of managing the disease for a time but that it was probably incurable. Statistically, the hope for a cure was probably less than a 5 percent chance.

After such news, some people may turn against God in anger, but thankfully I didn't experience that kind of frustration. I was devastated, no doubt, but I had nowhere else to turn. I never really asked, "Why me, Lord," so much as I asked, "What now, Lord? What's to become of my wife and son? How, dear Lord, will you provide for them?" Everywhere we turned, we were humbled to find that people were praying for us. We learned that one whole church of about five thousand had prayed for us in unison. So we prayed, too, that somehow the Lord would bring us through this, according to His perfect plan, no matter how incomprehensible such a "plan" might have seemed.

Had the Lord not prepared us well for such a time as this, I don't know how we could have gotten through the trials that followed. I immediately started chemotherapy in my hometown of Little Rock, where my father was a radiation oncologist and would become my greatest advocate and medical advisor. I was in the best of care—my father introduced me to "Doctor Jack," a brilliant medical oncologist and man of God who prayed with willing patients before tapping into their bloodstream to introduce his toxic remedies!

Yuko briefly returned to Japan, where our church members rallied around and helped her pack and ship what few possessions we could bring back to the United States. In His great goodness, the Lord provided the hugely supportive Fellowship Bible Church in Little Rock, where several of my doctors were also members. We joined a small group where Yuko and I became the focal point of the group's loving care. Everyone agreed that they had never had such a close-knit small group experience before, until they were presented with such a passionate cause to support. They loved on us, prayed for us, cried with us at times, and they brought meals, raked leaves, and painted walls when we finally settled into a little house of our own. More than anything, however, they prayed for us and with us.

Prayer was the key. I know that is the primary reason I am still here. And yet I do not presume upon God to suggest that anything we or anyone else could have done would bring about His healing. I will never understand why He chooses to heal some people and not others. It was a humbling lesson in just trusting the Lord to carry out His perfect will, knowing that I would somehow have to accept it even if He chose not to heal me. I believe this is where I found comfort, knowing that because it was beyond my control, for once I could fully trust in His plan and provision, regardless of what the future might hold.

Perhaps it's a personality thing as well—some people are okay with not knowing everything, just taking life as it comes. I've always enjoyed wandering down unmarked dirt roads that lead to heaven-knows-where—because joy, adventure, and new discoveries along the road can be found when you simply live for the moment. I found it easy to just rest in the Lord, trusting that He would show us the way.

I underwent conventional chemotherapy and eased into a couple of years of glorious remission. I learned how to give myself Interferon shots, which in those days promised some hope of prolonging the remission. Our little Sean learned that getting a shot wasn't so bad—he was a brave little fellow who brought untold joy into our lives. Every single day was priceless; every prayer we lifted up was so full of hope. Simple moments of laughter with Yuko and Sean were precious gifts that washed away the pain of intravenous solutions and toxic bags of "red devil chemo."

Three-year-old Sean was also the trooper who laughed while helping to shave my head when the recurrence finally happened a couple of years later. In some ways, the recurrence was even more devastating than the original diagnosis. Always the optimist, I was in denial by then, somehow hoping that it was all behind me. Yuko agreed that facing the same disease a second time was almost more than she could bear. Was this the end, we wondered?

Our small group rallied around and prayed over us again. I remember the night I literally cried in front of the group, and then cried out a desperate prayer: "Dear God, please let me live just long enough to see my son grow up to walk with you." One of my friends from the group told me some years later that hearing this prayer was hugely life-changing for him and gave him a whole new perspective on how precious our time is here on earth. I tried to remind myself that I had already lived a more blessed and interesting life in forty years than many people ever do in eighty. I had an adorable wife, a sweet young son, an intensely deep and rewarding walk with Jesus Christ, and had enjoyed a fascinating career that had taken me through dozens of countries around the world.

My perspective on a career was completely turned on its head. Where I had once lived out my identity as a global photojournalist, and took great pride in that, I had been humbled into giving it all up, literally overnight, and wondered if career would even matter in my future. "Would I even have a future?" I pondered. My identity in Christ became the new focus. Our faith, for both of us, was immeasurably deepened as our awareness of God's presence allowed us to have peace and hope despite the nearly hopeless odds.

What is God's plan in all this, we wondered, as we continued to pray for His will to be done. Oddly enough, we both began to realize that our desire for more children had never faded. We had been through five years of infertility before God blessed us with Sean, and now Sean was asking for a little brother. Between our prayers for Papa's healing, Sean's prayers for a brother took on a focused intensity that we could not ignore. With high-dose chemotherapy and a bone-marrow transplant on the horizon, our prayers shifted away from biological children to the possibility of adoption. Could this really be in God's plans for our family? What if I don't make it through the treatments? Is it wise to burden Yuko with another child if I'm not around to provide? How were we to make sense of all this?

In time, we understood that the longing in our hearts for another child was put there by God—it didn't make any sense otherwise. So we continued to pray about adoption, although we knew we didn't have the money to make it happen on our own.

In early 2000, I started the bone-marrow transplant with stem cells harvested from my own blood during remission. I was given high-dose chemotherapy that was toxic enough to completely destroy my bone marrow and all immune function, and then I came down with pneumonia and had no way to fight it off. The fever raged to about 105 degrees, and I drifted in and out of a hazy semiconscious state for a few days in the hospital. At times I was dimly aware of friends and pastors who came to my bedside and prayed over me. It seemed as if my father never left my side, making sure that everything that could be done was being done right.

Finally, during a fitful night of hallucinating dreams, I remember calling out to the Lord and praying all kinds of bargaining prayers. "I will truly commit the rest of my life to you," I bargained, "if you'll just pull me through this and let me live, dear Lord." I promised to surrender ALL of myself (there were parts of me I had wrongfully held onto and never fully surrendered over to the Lord). I laid it all out on the table, or across the bed, as it were. I remember emerging at one point from a fever-induced fog and having a very lucid moment of clarity. It was quite dark in my room, in the middle of the night. I envisioned an image of myself like a baby curled up in a fetal position, lying peacefully in the cupped palms of two very large hands. I heard a voice in my spirit that spoke clearly, unlike anything I had ever heard. "Trust me," He said, "Trust in me."

I am not from a church background where we tend to focus on emotional experiences or casually lay claim to supernatural encounters, but for the first time in my life I was certain that I heard God speak directly and clearly into my heart. A peace washed over me, and I drifted back to sleep. In the morning, I awoke to find that the fever had finally broken. It was a viral pneumonia rather than bacterial, so even the best antibiotics would not have helped. I simply had to survive this thing with no immune function of my own, but once again, the Lord was faithful to pull me through.

As I began to recover my strength in the coming months, our thoughts and prayers turned once again to adoption (little Sean's prayers for that had never wavered). Crazy as it seemed, we decided to trust that the Lord would help us accomplish the desire that only He could have put in our hearts. It was a process, and it took more time than just the adoption paperwork. I started a new job as a writer/editor in corporate marketing, so it took some time before we actually launched the adoption process.

It was also a faith step that we had to stew over for some time before we were ready to really take that leap.

As an international, bilingual family, the Lord really pulled our hearts toward international adoption. Very few places would consider us, because of my health history, so we finally settled on Russia. In the summer of 2003, we brought home a little one-year-old boy who we named Jesse Andrew Nelson.

Many people shared in the adoption experience with us through prayer and donations toward the costly fees and expenses. We were blessed with more than $10,000 from friends, family, and even a few anonymous donors toward the cause. Again, the Lord was faithful, and we just went along for the ride.

As a father, when I think seriously about the likelihood of whether I could passionately love someone else's child, it is overwhelming to realize that only God could put that kind of love into my heart so that I could share it with a little boy from halfway around the world.

The adoption experience alone could make for a good many more chapters on the Lord's faithfulness. I've included just part of the story here to reflect on how some things just don't make sense, aside from knowing that God simply has it all in His hands. He is always in control, even when it's impossible for us to understand His perfect plans. For this and so many other blessings, I can only be immensely thankful.

Believing in miracles, by His grace and mercy, I still walk in search of His plan.

*"Lord my God, I called to you for help,
and you healed me"*

(Psalms 30:2 NIV)

Chapter 4

Are You Willing to Pay the Price?

A re we willing to walk the same path to a deep walk with Him?

Jesus came to do the will of His Father—are we willing to do what He wills for us?

> *"Not everyone who says to me, 'Lord, Lord,' will enter the kingdom of heaven, but only the one who does the will of my Father who is in heaven."*
>
> *(Matthew 7:21 NIV)*

Are we willing to be filled with His Spirit? Do we want the same power to carry on the work Jesus did? If so, follow His teachings.

> *"But you will receive power when the Holy Spirit comes on you; and you will be my witnesses in Jerusalem, and in all Judea and Samaria, and to the ends of the earth."*
>
> *(Acts 1:8 NIV)*

> *"Do not get drunk on wine, which leads to debauchery. Instead, be filled with the Spirit."*
>
> *(Ephesians 5:18 NIV)*

Are we willing to pray without ceasing?

It seems that it's easy to indulge yourself in so many things of this world, which will cause your spiritual thought process to go into a dormant stage.

> *"Pray without ceasing. In everything give thanks, for this is the will of God in Christ Jesus toward you. Don't quench the Spirit."*
> (1 Thessalonians 5:17 WEB)

Are we willing to pray in the Spirit? If so, you will build up His Spirit within you.

Are you willing to intercede for others?

> *"He saw that there was no one;*
> *he was appalled that there was no one to intervene;*
> *so his own arm achieved salvation for him,*
> *and his own righteousness sustained him."*
> (Isaiah 59:16 NIV)

Are we willing to sacrifice a little sleep to pray? Jesus did—He spent nights in prayer.

Are we willing to spend time in His word and really get it into our spirits?

> *"My dear brothers and sisters, take note of this: Everyone should be quick to listen, slow to speak and slow to become angry, because human anger does not produce the righteousness that God desires. Therefore, get rid of all moral filth and the evil that is so prevalent and humbly accept the word planted in you, which can save you."*
> (James 1:19–21 NIV)

Are You Willing to Pay the Price?

This Scripture can save so many of us from a lot of pain, if we just take time to think and meditate on it before we speak.

> *"Therefore, I urge you, brothers and sisters, in view of God's mercy, to offer your bodies as a living sacrifice, holy and pleasing to God—this is your true and proper worship.² Do not conform to the pattern of this world, but be transformed by the renewing of your mind. Then you will be able to test and approve what God's will is—his good, pleasing and perfect will."*
>
> (Romans 12:1, 2 NIV)

Are we willing to discipline ourselves? Don't be conformed to the world but be transformed each day in Christ Jesus.

Set aside a regular time to pray and study, come what may. Keep working toward the mark. Chase after the prize. It's real. It's heaven.

Be willing to walk as Jesus did.

Ministry of reconciliation

> *"Therefore, I urge you, brothers and sisters, in view of God's mercy, to offer your bodies as a living sacrifice, holy and pleasing to God—this is your true and proper worship. Do not conform to the pattern of this world, but be transformed by the renewing of your mind. Then you will be able to test and approve what God's will is—His good, pleasing and perfect will."*
>
> (2 Corinthians 5:17-21 NIV)

Be ready and willing to do what God asked us to do. It's all about His Word! Study His Word to show yourself approved in His eyes.

Jesus was willing to do whatever it took to bring us back to God. He paid the ultimate price for us, and it was His earthly body.

Challenge yourself to be more like Him in your walk. I have known so many that truly have crucified their thoughts and actions daily to become one with Him.

Chapter 5

Christ Like

"Brenda Burton's" story by Russell Morrison

I was reading a small book by C S. Lewis about the case for Christianity. His book spoke a lot about good and bad behavior. His main focus was that behavior was not just from being taught. Good behavior came about from a higher source and his thoughts were that good behavior was from God.

I think once you find Jesus as your Lord, you want to share with others the joy that you have found. You want to change your behavior to be more like His. You want to help the poor, sick, lost, hungry, and those who are in prison.

Those are the traits Jesus wants His followers to have, and if you don't, you're following something else. My next door neighbor Brenda Burton and longtime friend has those Christ Like traits like no other. I'm not implying she walks on water and don't want to elevate her or place her on a pedestal, but she is on the right track. She has been involved in taking care of the poor in Benton Arkansas since I can remember. I asked her for a few stories for my book, and she brought over a few picture books and several nice things that were written about her volunteerism and I was just floored at how long she had been taking care of so many families in our small city.

One of the first things I asked her was, "What is one of your favorite Scriptures." She quoted Matthew 25:34–39.

> "Then the King will say to those on his right, 'Come, you who are blessed by my Father; take your inheritance, the kingdom prepared for you since the creation of the world. For I was hungry and you gave me something to eat, I was thirsty and you gave me something to drink, I was a stranger and you invited me in, I needed clothes and you clothed me, I was sick and you looked after me, I was in prison and you came to visit me.'
> "Then the righteous will answer him, 'Lord, when did we see you hungry and feed you, or thirsty and give you something to drink? When did we see you a stranger and invite you in or needing clothes and clothe you? When did we see you sick or in prison and go to visit you?"
> (Matthew 25:34–39 NIV)

Brenda has the same type of faith as the woman who touched the hem of Jesus' clothes and was healed. She pretty much has kept to a simple life so she could help others. She once noted to a friend one of Mother Teresa's quotes: "Let us live simply so that others may simply live."

I asked Brenda to give me a story for my book about her mission work and how God had blessed her on so many occasions. One story that she recalled was about a mother and daughter who came to the Care Center for help with just their daily needs. Most folks that came had many.

One mother told Brenda that she needed a high chair for her baby and at the same time one of the ladies needed a prom dress for her daughter.

Well, Brenda in one of her vivacious moods said she knew where there was a yard sale and thought she had seen a high chair earlier in the day. She told the group that she would make a quick trip to see if she could round up the things that were needed.

Once she arrived at the yard sale, Brenda found that the lady of the house had called it a day when she drove up. She knocked on the door and the lady said she was on the phone. Brenda asked if she could purchase the high chair in the yard, and the lady said, "You can have it." She also noticed a very pretty blue dress hanging in the garage that looked like a perfect choice for the young lady who was in need of a prom dress. She asked a second time for one more thing, and it was for the blue dress. The lady said, "You can have that too."

Brenda was beside herself thinking how great God was to help her with these small needs. These items were very much needed by these people who depended on Brenda for so much. Once getting back to her home, she told those that were waiting that she had brought back what they needed. They just praised God for taking care of their needs.

The girl who needed the dress, tried it on as soon as Brenda had brought it in the door, and it was a perfect fit! Wow! She was ready for the prom. This was no average teenage girl but one who had many challenges and was asked to go to the prom by a young man who had many of his own. Our wonderful loving Father in heaven gave them the opportunity to ride in a limo and have the same fun as so many kids without the limitation that had challenged these kids. The children that were in need along with so many hurdles did not slow Brenda and her faith down. There's not much that could slow her down from helping those in need.

I just found out a few months ago that Brenda, her husband, her sister, and her brother-in-law all attended a Bible study that Juanita taught. Brenda said that Juanita later helped them for a number of years with the Care Center where she and husband Dudley helped with the children. Juanita had such a heart for sharing with young people so they would have a good start on getting to know Jesus.

When God gives you a vision or a passion to do amazing things, don't let those dreams go to waste: go ahead and act on your faith. What does it mean to be Christ like? Look around each day and you will see those people acting like Jesus. They are sharing what they have with the poor, sick, and hungry. Take time to share what you have with others who are in need, and God will bless you for it.

> *"What good is it, my brothers and sisters, if someone claims to have faith but has no deeds? Can such faith save them? Suppose a brother or a sister is without clothes and daily food. If one of you says to them, "Go in peace; keep warm and well fed," but does nothing about their physical needs, what good is it? In the same way, faith by itself, if it is not accompanied by action, is dead.*
>
> *But someone will say, "You have faith; I have deeds."*
>
> *Show me your faith without deeds, and I will show you my faith by my deeds. You believe that there is one God. Good! Even the demons believe that—and shudder.*
>
> *You foolish person, do you want evidence that faith without deeds is useless? Was not our father Abraham considered righteous for what he did when he offered his son Isaac on the altar? You see that his faith and his actions were working together, and his faith was made complete by what he did. And the Scripture was fulfilled that says, "Abraham believed God, and it was credited to him as righteousness," and he was called*

God's friend. You see that a person is considered righteous by what they do and not by faith alone.

In the same way, was not even Rahab the prostitute considered righteous for what she did when she gave lodging to the spies and sent them off in a different direction? As the body without the spirit is dead, so faith without deeds is dead."

(James 2:14–26 NIV)

Thank God for men and women who listen to God's voice and go out and share with those that are in need.

Chapter 6

The Camping Trip that Changed My Life

"My Story" by Russell Morrison

"Whoever loves correction loves knowledge, but he who hates reproof is stupid."

(Proverbs:12:1NIV)

Early on I did not have the best attitude toward life and thought my life didn't seem to have much meaning or value. I embraced pessimism until a dear lady brought it to my attention. During this fun filled weekend I found out that pessimism was not a healthy life choice.

Around 1975 my wife and I celebrated the Fourth of July by enjoying a camping trip at one of the most spectacular lakes in the country. Ouachita Lake was named after the native Indians that lived in this area. Our dog, Sam the Sheltie, was along for the fun as well.

We had set up our small dome tent, and I was preparing a lunch on our hibachi grill. My wife had placed a few hot dogs on the grill, and we both took our eyes of the grill to enjoy the lovely view of the lake. Returning our attention to what we were cooking, we noticed that our sweet little dog had eaten just about all the hot dogs off the grill. He was not such a sweet little dog at that point of time. Back then we didn't have a whole lot of money for food, but we made do with what we packed to make up for the loss. We still were having the best times of our lives, and we were a young couple in love. We had a big laugh about how many hot dogs a small dog could eat. We still had a wonderful simple lunch minus the hot dogs.

After our tent was set up and our campsite ready to go for a weekend of fun camping, a very large RV pulling a fabulous boat, that must have been forty feet long, pulled up to our campsite. The driver poked his head out the window and said, "Hey, kids, we have been driving through all the camp sites and could not find a camping space. Is there any way we could share the campsite so we could spend this Fourth of July weekend camping without being on the side of the road? With our Arkansas hospitality we both agreed to share the campsite.

I did not have any idea how the weekend would change my life forever. What an exciting weekend for the both of us. They took us out on their boat both days and treated us like we were royalty.

During the hot summer evenings we would sit around and talk about various things that came up. The lady of the house (RV) must have really noticed my not-so-positive attitude and must have decided she had had enough of my mouth.

Every pessimistic word that came out of my mouth those days was like the smell of a toxic chemical dump.

She was not shy when she said that I was one of the most negative young men that she had ever met. She went on to tell me my view on life was not so good and that I needed to make a few changes. I didn't know at the time how to answer her except to talk a little about my childhood and how I was raised. But that is never an excuse for being so negative. I did grow up in a family of alcoholism, abuse, and mental illness. But again, this is no excuse for being such a butt, and I was one. So take advice from those that want to help you: improve who you are and take time to listen.

Well, to her that was no excuse either, for me to have such a bitter frame of mind, and that was what it was. From that night on I started looking at who I really was and what a miserable person I was. From that point on I can say thanks for such a wise lady. Just taking the time to share with me her thoughts about who she thought I was and giving me a little constructive criticism went a long way with me.

I was so blessed to have a person like her that I didn't even know to bring me into a more positive light. Well, that Texan gave me an idea that weekend that changed my life. I still work at it every day and will for the rest of my life. Wow! God is so good to place people like her into our lives. My wife had to deal with me for many years, and I was so glad she never gave up on the young man that was bitter at the world.

God was changing me from the inside out. He has had many years to mold this old piece of clay into a more mature Christian. I know that His hands are still molding and shaping me into a vessel that can be used to help others.

Another lady in my life who helped to mold and instruct me was my mother-in-law. Back in the seventies she had such a positive attitude on life and would share with us young Christians who seemed to be in search for a meaningful life.

The power of love and faith in this woman seemed to stir my most inner spiritual person. I was starting to change again. It was not soon enough for my young bride, but she hung in there.

The study of God's Word seemed to inspire me to look in the mirror and change the person I was. I have been through much loss in my life, and I will not let things around me cause the negative person to come back in. I wasn't going to wake up and start being the old negative person again. I will not let him come back in. I think people who are negative must be some of the most miserable people in the world. I was.

In the past I have had the misfortune to work with some of the most negative people in the world. I am so blessed in my current job at Arkansas Heart Hospital to work with some of the most positive people in the world. It helps to be around positive people. Always take a look at yourself and see if you have some negative thing to say about your coworker, boss, job, or wife. If you can't go a day without saying something positive about them, take another look at yourself. Start believing the best in people and see what happens. Take time in your day to say a simple prayer and ask God to help change your negative thinking habits. My wife and mother-in-law must have said a few prayers, which, along with a sweet lady from Texas, brought me to my knees.

The ear that listens to reproof lives, and will be at home among the wise.
(Proverbs 15:31 WEB)

One word Juanita noted in her journals was the word wisdom, and she routinely prayed for her family and friends. She wanted her family to use wisdom in making the right decisions in their lives. When you make wise choices in your life, everything becomes much easier, and all seems to flow with the current of life and not against the current of life, which can be very hard.

All she wanted her friend's family to do is use common sense and ask God to help us make the right choices. Many people want to blame other people or their parents for the bad choices that they made. It could be time to wake up and look in the mirror.

Chapter 7

Confession Brings Life

September 28, 1984

Faith and confession and the power of the tongue were noted in Juanita's journal.

> "Death and life are in the power of the tongue.
> And those that love it will eat its fruit."
>
> (Proverbs 18:21 WEB)

> "It is the spirit who gives life. The flesh profits nothing. The words that I speak to you are spirit, and are life."
>
> (John 6:63 WEB)

> "The good man out of the good treasure of his heart brings out that which is good, and the evil man out of the evil treasure of his heart brings out that which is evil, for out of the abundance of the heart, his mouth speaks."
>
> (Luke 6:45 WEB)

A good man of a good treasure brings good. We need to produce spiritual fruit. If you are not in Christ, who are you standing with?

> *"We all stumble in many ways. Anyone who is never at fault in what they say is perfect, able to keep their whole body in check.*
>
> *When we put bits into the mouths of horses to make them obey us, we can turn the whole animal. Or take ships as an example. Although they are so large and are driven by strong winds, they are steered by a very small rudder wherever the pilot wants to go. Likewise, the tongue is a small part of the body, but it makes great boasts. Consider what a great forest is set on fire by a small spark. The tongue also is a fire, a world of evil among the parts of the body. It corrupts the whole body, sets the whole course of one's life on fire, and is itself set on fire by hell.*
>
> *All kinds of animals, birds, reptiles and sea creatures are being tamed and have been tamed by mankind, but no human being can tame the tongue. It is a restless evil, full of deadly poison.*
>
> *With the tongue we praise our Lord and Father, and with it we curse human beings, who have been made in God's likeness. Out of the same mouth come praise and cursing. My brothers and sisters, this should not be. Can both fresh water and salt water flow from the same spring? My brothers and sisters, can a fig tree bear olives, or a grapevine bear figs? Neither can a salt spring produce fresh water."*
>
> (James 3:2–12 NIV)

Man must bridle his tongue. Take control of what you say.

What I put in my heart will come out of my mouth.

Watching what we say is good medicine for our bodies, which will produce healing. *My tongue has gotten me into a lot of trouble over the years and I'm working on what I say each and every day. When I listen first and think clearly about what I'm going to say before I engage my mouth, the right words are brought forth. I have found out that a positive word is much healthier than one that is negative and will bring results that are positive and will help make us successful in all things.*

Take God's Word for spiritual healing. This will bring physical healing to your body.

> *"My son, pay attention to what I say; turn your ear to my words. Do not let them out of your sight; keep them within your heart; for they are life to those who find them and health to one's whole body. Above all else, guard your heart, for everything you do flows from it. Keep your mouth free of perversity; keep corrupt talk far from your lips."*
>
> (Proverbs 4:20-24 NIV)

The word of God is medicine to my flesh. The word of the world is power to your flesh.

> *"Give thanks to the LORD, for he is good; his love endures forever.*
>
> (Psalm 107:1 NIV)

> *"So is my word that goes out from my mouth:
> It will not return to me empty,
> but will accomplish what I desire
> and achieve the purpose for which I sent it."*
>
> (Isaiah 55:11 NIV)

Say the Word of God. Believe the Word and you can be made whole.

Juanita believed that we can receive healing from God by believing in His Word and that by faith the Holy Spirit would permeate our body and we would be healed. I believe the Holy Spirit speaks to us through our spirits so we can be receptive to Him.

> *"For most certainly I tell you, whoever may tell this mountain, 'Be taken up and cast into the sea,' and doesn't doubt in his heart, but believes that what he says is happening; he shall have whatever he says. Therefore I tell you, all things whatever you pray and ask for, believe that you have received them, and you shall have them. Whenever you stand praying, forgive, if you have anything against anyone; so that your Father, who is in heaven, may also forgive you your transgressions. But if you do not forgive, neither will your Father in heaven forgive your transgressions."*
> (Mark 11:23–26 WEB)

Whatever we say and believe we will have. It is a mind set on Jesus that will change your life.

Hope is the goal setter for us.

> *"Who in hope believed against hope, to the end that he might become a father of many nations, according to that which had been spoken, so shall thy seed be. And without being weakened in faith he considered his own body now as good as dead (he being about a hundred years old), and the deadness of Sarah's womb."*
> (Romans 4:18–19 WEB)

Sarah's hope caused her to become a mother of many nations.

We call what is not as though it were and that is called faith.

Acknowledge the facts but consider the promise.

Hope is the future.

> *"Hope deferred makes the heart sick,
> but a longing fulfilled is a tree of life."*
>
> (Proverbs 13:12 NIV)

> *"Through whom we have gained access by faith into this grace in which we now stand. And we boast in the hope of the glory of God. Not only so, but we also glory in our sufferings, because we know that suffering produces perseverance; perseverance, character; and character, hope. And hope does not put us to shame, because God's love has been poured out into our hearts through the Holy Spirit, who has been given to us."*
>
> (Romans 5:2–5 NIV)

Experience brings hope into what we are experiencing in our daily lives.

> *"For in this hope we were saved. But hope that is seen is no hope at all. Who hopes for what they already have? But if we hope for what we do not yet have, we wait for it patiently."*
>
> (Romans 8:24 NIV)

Wait for it and do not lose hope: we will win this race of faith.

> *"Now faith is assurance of things hoped for, a conviction of things not seen."*
>
> (Hebrews 11:1 KJV)

Faith will not work without hope. Remember that faith is the substance of things hoped for.

"By faith I have it now." *Juanita believed God would take care of every need in her life. She believed that those things that you don't see are eternal, and those things that we see are not. Her deep study of the Bible caused her to believe by her faith and not by her sight.*

Chapter 8

Walking In the Spirit

Walking in the spirit will keep you from walking in the flesh. It is being led by the Holy Spirit that will cause us to be like Him.

> *"Those who belong to Christ Jesus have crucified the flesh with its passions and desires. Since we live by the Spirit, let us keep in step with the Spirit."*
>
> (Galatians 5:24–25 NIV)

What does the Lord want of us?

1. To love Him. To put Him in control of our lives so that He has complete control of our desires. Our desires have gotten in the way of loving Him and letting Him have complete control.

   > *"This is my commandment, that you love one another, even as I have loved you."*
   >
   > (John 15:12 WEB)

2. To love one another. *Don't let petty differences and insignificant things slow you down, which will keep you from loving one another. Let*

resentment and hate go. *This is not what the body of Christ is like. We need to love one another as Jesus loved us so we can walk the same walk of love Jesus did. Loving those that run over you and trying to control every move you make can be very hard. Again what does the Word/Bible tell you to do? Love one another—and that is what we need to work toward.*

3. Be obedient to His word and His will. *One word that is hard for most of us is the word obedience. Most of us don't want anything to do with being obedient to anyone or anything. Take the time out of your day to say a prayer or to study His Word. That is a good step toward that one word, which most of us fear, obedience.*

"Jesus replied, "Anyone who loves me will obey my teaching. My Father will love them, and we will come to them and make our home with them."

(John 14:23 NIV)

This Scripture is so right on. We need to keep His Word. One way for us to truly find out who God is, is by taking time to pray and meditate on His Word. By doing this we will have an open communication and will be able to grow into His likeness.

4. Bear the fruit of the Holy Spirit.

"But the fruit of the Spirit is love, joy, peace, forbearance, kindness, goodness, faithfulness, gentleness and self-control. Against such things there is no law. Those who belong to Christ Jesus have crucified the flesh with its passions and desires. Since we live by the Spirit, let us keep in step with the Spirit. Let us not become conceited, provoking and envying each other."

(Galatians 5:22–26 NIV)

These are the attributes that you'll possess when you walk in the Spirit and not in the flesh.

(1) Love
(2) Joy
(3) Peace
(4) Patience
(5) Kindness
(6) Goodness
(7) Faithfulness
(8) Humility
(9) Meekness
(10) Self-control

These are the examples of real fruit on the tree of our spiritual man. People can determine what kind of person you really are by the type of fruit that you produce in your life.

Exercise your faith. Without faith it is impossible to please God. *I heard this from Juanita on many occasions.*

Walking in the spirit of Jesus is letting Jesus have complete control of each and every step you take in this life.

It is not an up-and-down walk because when Jesus is in control, it is an even flow and a precious walk with our Lord.

Walk toward the spiritual high ground and stay out of the valleys.

How can you do that? By prayer, study, and being plugged in to His Word.

Don't let the enemy pull you down and don't let the things of this world slow down your walk of faith.

The Lord is our Shepherd. He will lead us into a calmer life and will guide us by His spiritual light.

Our goal as Christians is to be gentle, quiet, and peaceful, with quiet assurance and never a condemner.

> *"I have told you these things, so that in me you may have peace. In this world you will have trouble. But take heart! I have overcome the world."*
> (John 16:33 NIV)

> *"Therefore, there is now no condemnation for those who are in Christ Jesus, because through Christ Jesus the law of the Spirit who gives life has set you free from the law of sin and death."*
> (Roman 8:1–2 NIV)

Watch for the enemy outside, and walk in God's Spirit and not in the flesh.

> *"The thief comes only to steal and kill and destroy; I have come that they may have life, and have it to the full."*
> (John 10:10 NIV)

Satan roars into our lives with a loud voice, confusion, fear, and anxiety and wants our personal lives to be disrupted. Jesus is the one who gives us our strength and is the One who helps us to be champions as we fight those spiritual battles that come our way.

> *"For the Spirit God gave us does not make us timid, but gives us power, love and self-discipline."*
> (2 Timothy 1:7 NIV)

"But those who hope in the Lord will renew their strength. They will soar on wings like eagles; they will run and not grow weary, they will walk and not be faint."

(Isaiah 40:31 NIV)

They will walk, and not faint was a Scripture that Juanita quoted for herself and all of her family. She quoted this wonderful Scripture every day, living to be eighty-three.

Wait on the Lord and He will give you the strength that you need in any situation in life. Just keep on trusting in Him. This Scripture was one of Juanita's favorites. We will mount up with wings like eagles and not be weary or faint.

"The Spirit himself testifies with our spirit that we are God's children."

(Romans 8:16 NIV)

Chapter 9

Obedience

Obedience: to submit to; to yield to; to surrender to

Obey: to comply with orders

Jesus was obedient. Philippians 2:8 (KJV) says, "And being found in fashion as a man, he humbled himself, and became obedient unto death, even the death of the cross." Jesus, our example, was obedient to His Father even unto death. Everything Jesus did was an act of obedience to His Father.

> *"As obedient children, not fashioning yourselves according to the former lusts in your ignorance: but as he which hath called you is holy, so be ye holy in all manner of living. Because it is written, Be ye holy, for I am holy."*
> (1 Peter 1: 14–16 KJV)

Obedience is surrendering and submitting to our Heavenly Father. And, yes, for most of us it is a very hard thing to commit to believing that God will take care of us and He is real and He will actually help us through each day.

"And it shall come to pass, if thou shalt hearken diligently unto the voice of the LORD thy God, to observe and to do all his commandments which

I command thee this day, that the LORD thy God will set thee on high above all nations of the earth:."

(Deuteronomy 28:1 KJV)

We are blessed when we are obedient. Obedience comes just because we love and because we desire to please our Father. How do we learn obedience?

To grow in faith, we must listen to the voice of the Holy Spirit and then by studying God's Word.

One word that most people do not like to hear is obedience. If you want to grow as a person work on being obedient and listen to those around you that can help you grow in grace.

Obedience:

1. Acting on His Word. Taking God's Word and doing exactly what it says.
2. Listening to His voice. Jesus said, "My sheep will know my voice.' Peace—that you will know on the inside.
3. Stepping out by faith. To let the gifts of the Spirit operate through us: Word of knowledge; healing; message in tongues.
4. Surrendering and letting God use us in His way.

Jesus said, "All I want to do is the will of the Father."

What are some things God has been telling us?

1. Be holy
2. Fast and Pray
3. Intercede

4. Visit the sick, the orphans, and the widows
5. Cast out devils

"When I was a child, I spoke as a child, I felt as a child, I thought as a child. Now that I have become a man, I have put away childish things. For now we see in a mirror, dimly, but then face to face. Now I know in part, but then I will know fully, even as I was also fully known. But now faith, hope, and love remain—these three. The greatest of these is love."

(1 Corinthians 13:11–13 WEB)

I was thumbing through my daughter's Bible many years after she had passed away from fighting a very long battle with cancer and found some sermon notes she had taken while she was attending our church. The sermon was called "Lead, Follow, or Get Out of the Way."

Men who get out of the way:

1. Have not embraced their relationship with Christ and His Word
2. Have "checked out" and neglect their responsibilities
3. Are selfish and self-centered
4. Have no real purpose in life
5. Biblical character—Jonah: "But Jonah ran away from the Lord and headed for Tarshish. He went down to Joppa where he found a ship bound for that port. After paying the fare, he went aboard and sailed for Tarshish to flee from the Lord." (Jonah 1:3 KJV)

Men who follow their own desires:

1. Have not embraced their relationship with Christ and His word
2. Do not understand their role in the home

3. Are easily swayed (live by natural tendencies)
4. Biblical charter—Peter: "Peter asked, 'Lord, why can't I follow you now? I will lay down my life for you.' Then Jesus answered. "Will you really lay down your life for me? I tell you the truth, before the rooster crows, you will disown me three times!" (John 13:37, 38 NIV)

Men who lead:

1. Have embraced their relationship with Christ and His word

2. Take responsibility for their life

3. Serve others

4. Know where they are going

5. Biblical character—Paul:

   "Brothers and sisters, I do not consider myself yet to have taken hold of it. But one thing I do: Forgetting what is behind and straining toward what is ahead, press on toward the goal to win the prize for which God has called me heavenward in Christ Jesus."
   (Philippians 3:13, 14 NIV)

6. Men need to lead or just get out of the way.

Men, we need to challenge each other to lead our families in the right walk. But whatever you do, put childish ways behind you, take responsibility, and lead your family! Be obedient before God—it will change who you are.

Obedience

"If you fully obey the LORD your God and carefully follow all his commands I give you today, the LORD your God will set you high above all the nations on earth. All these blessings will come on you and accompany you if you obey the LORD your God."

(Deuteronomy 28:1–2 NIV)

I can say that I have not been very obedient in my walk with God during my life. I could have done much more than I have done with my walk with Him. Most of my life I've just been a spiritual bystander and let others take care of things I should have. I have felt on several occasions that I was being led by His Spirit to do something for God. I acted on some but let many opportunities pass by.

I feel like I have been motivated by the Holy Spirit to write these two books and have been so compelled each day to grow in the knowledge of God's Word. I feel very much consumed by learning something new each day. Just by reading Juanita's journals each day has changed the way I look at life.

Chapter 10

Intercessory Prayer

"And he saw that there was no man, and wondered that there was no intercessor."

(Isaiah 59:16 WEB)

*A*nyone who was around Juanita for a short period of time would realize that there was something very special about her when it came to her prayer life. After meeting Juanita for the first time most of us knew that she would be placing you on her prayer list and that she would be interceding for you before the day ended.

I found an entire journal listing those friends and family members for whom she was praying. She was very specific about what she was praying for. If you needed prayer for healing, wisdom or just a little peace in your life, she would add your name and then ask God to help you with what she believed was causing you to fall short with your spiritual walk. If you had any kind of issue in your life she would write your name down and start praying for you and she would not stop. She had a few individuals that she kept on her list and I'm very glad I was one of them.

> *"And I sought for a man among them that I should make up the hedge and stand in the gap before me for the land, that I should not destroy it: but I found none."*
>
> (Ezekiel 22:30 KJV)

Intercessor—is a person who is a go-between, one who gets God's attention on behalf of a person, persons, or a place. *Juanita was that person of faith that took time daily to pray for us.*

An intercessor stands in the gap. Intercessory prayer takes a type of *agape* love.

One thing we need is agape love. Agape is not limited to God's love of humanity; it can also be used to describe the love one person has for another. In contrast to the sexual type of love, agape love describes a selfless kind of love that involves giving without expectation of anything in return.

Moses was an intercessor. He stood in the gap for Israel. God is looking for intercessors to stand in the gap today—to pray, to intercede. *Juanita was one of those prayer warriors who always stood in the gap for those who were in need of her prayers. I know she kept on her knees in her prayer closet asking God to answer her requests to help those in need. I heard a preacher once who said that our prayer warriors are dying off and going to heaven and what will the world be like when that happens. Well it is happening and if we as Christians don't get serious about our prayer life it won't get better.*

Intercessory Prayer

> *"I exhort [admonish and urge], therefore, that, first of all, supplications, prayers, intercessions, and giving of thanks, be made for all men; For kings, and for all that are in authority [high place: our president,*

governor, etc.]; that we may lead a quiet and peaceable life in all godliness and honesty. For this is good and acceptable in the sight of God our Savior."

(1 Timothy 2:1, 2 WEB)

"Intercession is many times an agonizing travailing in our spirit as we intercede. Paul says, "My little children of whom I travail in birth again until Christ be formed in you" [labor pains]."

(Galatians 4:19 KJV)

"In the same way, the Spirit helps us in our weakness. We do not know what we ought to pray for, but the Spirit himself intercedes for us through wordless groans."

(Romans 8:26 NIV)

Travailing—Praying in the Spirit—Praying in tongues: It is as God gives us a burden to intercede. We may not know how to pray, and as we begin to pray in tongues or in the Spirit, we travail.

We should be specific when we intercede. Call that person, county, nation, or family by name. Paul prayed:

"For this cause we also, since the day we heard it, do not cease to pray for you, and to desire that ye might be filled with the knowledge of his will in all wisdom and spiritual understanding; that ye might walk worthy of the Lord unto all pleasing, being fruitful in every good work, and increasing in the knowledge of God; strengthened with all might, according to his glorious power, unto all patience and longsuffering with joyfulness; giving thanks unto the Father, which hath made us meet to be partakers of the inheritance of the saints in the light."

(Colossians 1:9–12 KJV)

Intercession will not work without the Holy Spirit. Jesus was filled with the Holy Ghost.

> *"In the same way, the Spirit helps us in our weakness. We do not know what we ought to pray for, but the Spirit himself intercedes for us through wordless groans."*
>
> (Romans 8:26 NIV)

True intercessions will result in revival—an outpouring of the Holy Spirit.

> *"They all joined together constantly in prayer, along with the women and Mary the mother of Jesus, and with his brothers."*
>
> (Acts. 1:14 NIV)

In Acts 2:7 all were filled with the Holy Ghost. Revival broke out. Peter began to preach and 3,000 were saved.

Intercession will not work without a clean, sanctified body. *We need to push the sin out of our lives. Sin is just doing the wrong thing over and over again, which makes us pretty miserable when we do it. Down deep we all know what is right and what is wrong. But the flesh keeps coming at us until we succumb to something that we shouldn't do. One word that will help you succeed is the word meditation. Meditate on His Word and things will change for the better.*

> *"As for other matters, brothers and sisters, we instructed you how to live in order to please God, as in fact you are living. Now we ask you and urge you in the Lord Jesus to do this more and more. For you know what instructions we gave you by the authority of the Lord Jesus."*
>
> (1 Thessalonians 4:1 WEB)

"Do you not know that your bodies are temples of the Holy Spirit, who is in you, whom you have received from God? You are not your own; you were bought at a price. Therefore honor God with your bodies."
(1 Corinthians 6:19, 20 NIV)

"Put on the whole armor of God: "Put on the full armor of God, so that you can take your stand against the devil's schemes."
(Ephesians 6:11 NIV)

When we come to prayer—intercessory or whatever kind of prayer—the devil sure doesn't want us going into God's throne room. He will try to prevent it. So clothe yourself in the full armor; clothe yourself for battle and go to prayer and stay in the Word.

Pray in the Spirit and pray in your understanding. Spirit is tongues. Understanding is your own language.

"So what shall I do? I will pray with my spirit, but I will also pray with my understanding; I will sing with my spirit, but I will also sing with my understanding."
(1 Corinthians 14:15 NIV)

"Intercede and pray for your enemies. "But I tell you, love your enemies and pray for those who persecute you."
(Matthew 5:44 NIV)

In developing the character of an intercessor, Jesus is our example.

1. Have a regular time of prayer and intercessory prayer.

2. Prayer keeps us from temptation.

3. We must withdraw ourselves alone (go to our prayer closet).

4. As we get in prayer, we find out God's will. We get out of us and into Him.

5. Agonizing—travailing. James 5:16 says, "The effectual fervent prayer of a righteous man availeth much." (KJV)

6. Be sensitive to the leading of the Holy Spirit.

7. Our countenance is changed as we pray and intercede.

   "And it came to pass about eight days after these sayings, he took Peter and John and James, and went up into a mountain to pray. And as he prayed, the fashion of his countenance was altered, and his raiment was white and glistening."

   (Luke 9:28, 29 KJV)

8. Meditate and pray so you can enter into God's Glory, so you can take part in His plan for your life.

Chapter 11

We Have the Right to Use the Name of Jesus

We have the right and the authority to use the name of Jesus. Ephesians 3:14–15 (KJV) says, "For this cause I bow my knees unto the Father of our Lord Jesus Christ, of whom the whole family in heaven and earth is named." It is not important which church you belong but to which *family* you belong. The name of Jesus is given to the family of God our Father. Many people know about praying to God but not anything about praying to the Father because they don't really know Him.

He is God to the World but Father to me and to you. If you have accepted Jesus as Lord and Savior, he is your Father. He hears our prayers and answers our prayers. His Word says we are to ask the Father in the name of Jesus. Jesus is the authority and the name we use. We can take the name of Jesus and break the power of Satan over our loved ones that are not saved. "In the Name of the Lord Jesus Christ, I break the power of the devil over my friend in Christ and I claim his or her salvation."

"Teacher," said John, "we saw someone driving out demons in your name and we told him to stop, because he was not one of us."

"Do not stop him," Jesus said. "For no one who does a miracle in my name can in the next moment say anything bad about me, for whoever is not against us is for us. Truly I tell you, anyone who gives you a cup of water in my name because you belong to the Messiah will certainly not lose their reward."

(Mark: 9:38–50 NIV)

"Jesus called his twelve disciples to him and gave them authority to drive out impure spirits and to heal every disease and sickness."

(Mathew 10:1 NIV)

"Heal the sick who are there and tell them, "The kingdom of God has come near to you."

(Luke 10:9 NIV)

Your body may be bound with sickness. Say, "Satan, I break your power over my life and body, and I claim deliverance and healing in Jesus' name." See, we break and loose the devil's holding with the all-powerful name of Jesus. Now, thank God, his hold is broken. Thank God for salvation, healing, or whatever you have claimed.

One thing I remember most about my mother-in-law is that she studied these ancient writings that are more than 2,000 years old that the world and millions call the Bible. She took everything in the Bible and declared them all in the name of Jesus. She would proclaim everything in the name of Jesus. You are healed. You are going to have that job and that promotion. I sure could use her mighty prayers now.

You know, I can't believe I just wrote those few lines, that "I could use her mighty words of prayer." I have the same faith that she did, and guess what—many of those prayers that I have prayed have come to pass. I seem to forget how blessed

We Have the Right to Use the Name of Jesus

I am and that my prayers, like the prayers of many others, have been answered because I believe they will be. God bless Juanita for leaving such a positive impression on me and on my family.

Who is the one out there that is the positive influence that you're observing. Someone is watching us all the time. Be a good steward and be an example to others. Another area of my life I need to work on is truly trusting in my own faith in God.

What she was trying to tell all of us was that we should just believe in God and trust His Word, and His Word will help you through any situation that comes your way. Just believe in Him in all aspects of your life and those things that seem impossible will become possible.

Praying daily has come very natural for me throughout my life and I don't mind asking God to help in any situation or need that I might have. I, like many Christians, believe that we should treat God as our heavenly Father who cares for His children and gives them the desires of their hearts.

I remember that I prayed as a young boy that God would deliver me from the insanity of my dysfunctional family that I was born into, that caused me a lot of stress. I needed a home in which I didn't have to fear for my life daily. I just wanted a home that was peaceful, happy, and without the madness that might come through the door at any time of the day or night. My mother decided to leave my dad and relocate to the great state of Arkansas. I can remember praying for a wife as a young man and a family of my own.

I think we should write down what we are praying for and again be specific. Since that prayer I have been married for forty years now and have been blessed with a great wife, two kids, three grandchildren, and a daughter-in-law who are all very special in my life.

Chapter 12

God's Reason for Creation

God is a master designer. As we look at the beautiful creation of the heavens and the earth, we know that is exactly what God is. Why did He create all of this? *Was there an Intelligent Designer behind all of this? Yes there was, and He is the almighty programmer who put the entire world's together and we were made in His image believe it or not.*

He wanted to provide an appropriate place or environment for man. God, in His plan, created all resources, everything that man would ever need, and He did this for the man and woman. Science has tried to figure it all out, and they are trying to do it with sense knowledge.

Sense knowledge is the knowledge derived from our five senses: seeing, hearing, touching, smelling, and tasting. *You can look at me and tell that taste has caused me a lot of trouble.* God is a spirit, and we must worship Him in spirit and truth. Man has been unable to know God because God is a spirit and man was alienated from God until we came to know Jesus. We cannot find God with our five senses. God is a spirit, and God must reveal Himself to man. He has given us revelation knowledge for us to use to grow closer to Him. He sent Jesus to reveal Himself to us. He gave us the revelation knowledge of Himself to our recreated spirits by His Word.

"For what man knoweth the things of a man, save the spirit of man which is in him? Even so the things of God knoweth no man, but the Spirit of God. Now we have received, not the spirit of the world, but the spirit which is of God; that we might know the things that are freely given to us of God. Which things also we speak, not in the words which man's wisdom teacheth, but which the Holy Spirit teaches; comparing spiritual things with spiritual. But the natural man receiveth not the things of the Spirit of God: for they are foolishness unto him."

(Ephesians 3:14–15 KJV)

The Bible is God's revelation to man. He has put His inner thoughts and purposes down in His Word. It is His revelation to us in the world (sense knowledge—revelation knowledge).

One question that all of mankind has been asking since the beginning of time and that is, why did God create the heaven and earth? The Bible said it was for man and that the heavens were created for the earth.

"And God said, Let there be light in the firmament of the heaven to divide the day from the night; and let them be for signs, and for seasons, and for days, and years: And let them be for light in the firmament of the heaven to give light upon the earth: and it was so. And God made two great lights; the greater light to rule the day, and the lesser light to rule the night: he made the stars also. And God set them in the firmament of the heaven to give light upon the earth, to rule over the day and over the night, and to divide the light from the darkness: and God saw that it was good."

(Genesis 1:14–18 WEB)

The heavens are earth's only perfect timepiece. The seasons, signs, etc. were for the earth.

God's Reason for Creation

The reason for earth was man. God desired fellowship and love. He desired someone to pour out blessings upon. God created a beautiful earth and the reason for all of the creation was man. He was preparing a place for man. He provided every need for man in the earth: food, beauty, resources, and even a few jewels to brighten our lives a little.

> *"For thus saith the Lord that created the heavens; God himself that formed the earth and made it; he hath established it, he created it not in vain,"* (Isaiah 45:18 KJV) *And He formed it to be inhabited.*

Man is the only creature who can truly enjoy the earth's beauty and its resources that we all share.

The reason for man is the Father—the heart of God. The reason for the heavens is the earth. The reason for the earth is man.

> *"In the beginning God (Elohim—reveals the Trinity—God, Jesus, and the Holy Spirit) created the heavens and the earth."*
> (Genesis 1:1)

> *"In the beginning was the Word, and the Word was with God, and the Word was God. The same was in the beginning with God. All things were made by him; and without him was not anything made that was made."*
> (John 1:1–3 KJV)

> *This is what the brilliant minds call "intelligent design." There was a great designer behind all that was created, and it was God.*

> *"And the earth was without form, and void; and darkness was upon the face of the deep. And the Spirit of God moved upon the face of the waters."*
> (Genesis 1:2 KJV)

> "And Jesus, when he was baptized, went up straightway out of the water: and, lo, the heavens were opened unto him, and he saw the Spirit of God descending like a dove, and lighting upon him: And lo a voice from heaven, saying, This is my beloved Son, in whom I am well pleased."
>
> (Matthew 3:16, 17 KJV)

The Trinity was revealed to the senses of man. Man could hear the voice, and could see Jesus and the Spirit.

> "According as he hath chosen us in him before the foundation of the world, that we should be holy and without blame before him in love."
>
> (Ephesians 1:4 KJV)

The nature of God desired fellowship—sons and daughters to love, to talk to, to commune with. He created a place and then created man and women. He created us in His image, to want children to love. God is omnipotent. God is omnipresent. God is a Father God. His loving nature is His children. God cares for His children.

> "If ye then, being evil, know how to give good gifts unto your children, how much more shall your Father which is in heaven give good things to them who ask him?"
>
> (Matthew 7:11 KJV)

As we get our mind renewed with the Word of God, we can become conscious of the Father nature of God.

The attributes of God: God is a Father God. God is a Love God. God is a Faith God. Love caused Him to create the universe, and He created it by faith.

God's Reason for Creation

God created man in His own image to fellowship with Him and to love Him. He planned and created the beautiful home for His child.

> *"And God said; let us make man in our image, after our likeness."*
> (Genesis 1:26 KJV)

Man must be created as near like His creation in order to be God's child and heir. Our children are created to be like us. God's children are created to be like Him.

> *"And the Lord God formed man of the dust of the ground, and breathed into his nostrils the breath of life; and man became a living soul."*
> (Genesis 2:7 KJV)

> *"And the very God of peace sanctify you wholly; and I pray God your whole spirit and soul and body be preserved blameless unto the coming of our Lord Jesus Christ."*
> (1 Thessalonians 5:23 KJV)

God created man as a being, and this means we have a spirit—this is the real us, the real man created in the image of God. We have a soul, which is our reasoning power—our mind, emotions, and will. Our spirit and soul are housed in a body. Our soul and body are the instruments through which our spirit, the real us, operates.

Man was created a spirit to walk on the level with His Father God. God is a spirit. The Holy Spirit and angels are spiritual beings. Satan and his demons are spiritual beings. God gave to man a will. The will of man has the power of choice. We can choose to live for God or not. We have the choice. He gave to us the responsibility to choose to love Him and fellowship with Him. God gave man a mind, a very intellectual mind, a wise mind.

> "And out of the ground the Lord God formed every beast of the field, and every fowl of the air; and brought them unto Adam to see what he would call them: and whatsoever Adam called every living creature, that was the name thereof. And Adam gave names to all cattle, and the fowl of the air and to every beast of the field; but for Adam there was not found a helpmeet for him."
>
> (Genesis 1:28 KJV)

Adam, the first man had to be highly intelligent to name all the things of creation. Remember, the reason for man's existence is the Father, God's desire for fellowship with man.

Therefore, man's mental capacities were such that his mind could fellowship with the mind of His creator. When man was created, he was perfect. His spirit was eternal, and His body in the beginning was created to be eternal. Sin got in the way, and imperfection came in and took him down.

God gave man authority and dominion over everything that He created.

> "And God blessed them, and God said unto them, be fruitful, and multiply, and replenish the earth, and subdue it: and have dominion over the fish of the sea, and over the fowl of the air, and over every living thing that moveth upon the earth."
>
> (Genesis 1:28 KJV)

> "For thou has made him a little lower than [God—Elohim] the angels, and hast crowned him with glory and honor."
>
> (Psalm 8:5 KJV)

Man was an eternal spirit-being in God's class with an eternal human body. Adam's was given this world to rule but failed.

> *"But there is a place where someone has testified: "What is mankind that you are mindful of them, a son of man that you care for him? You made them a little lower than the angels;*
>
> *you crowned them with glory and honor and put everything under their feet."*
>
> *In putting everything under them, God left nothing that is not subject to them Yet at present we do not see everything subject to them."*
>
> (Hebrews 2:6-8 KJV)

Adam ruled creation by his word. His voice was like the voice of God. In his dominion over creation Adam had such complete authority over everything that he had the legal right to turn it over to someone else, and he did that very thing.

Adam—the first man God created. He was responsible for:

1. Fellowshipping with God and bringing God joy
2. Bringing the human family into the world
3. Bringing spiritual men and women into the world to give God heirs to His kingdom and to worship Him and give Him pleasure

This seems pretty far out from how most people think today, that is, that man was created to communicate with a higher being or intelligent designer. We do have a mind of our own that can reason and a mind that says we can choose how we want to believe, and it is wonderful that we have a choice and a free will to believe in any way we want. I'm like millions of people in this world who will continue to believe that we were made in His image and by the great Designer that we call God.

Genesis 1:28 teaches us that God made Adam and Eve fellow workers with Him in bringing the human family into the world.

Man's real business in the beginning was to give birth to God's children, and that is what our real business is too—to share God's love and witness by bringing new children into God's Kingdom. Man gives birth to eternal children who will live as long as God lives.

We are spirit beings. Our spirit beings will never die.

> *"The first man Adam was made a living soul; the last Adam [Christ] was made a quickening [life giving] spirit."*
>
> (1 Corinthians 15:45 NIV)

God created Adam and Eve perfect. He gave them dominion over all God's creation. They fellowshipped with God, and God said, "There is only one thing you can't do: Don't eat of the tree of knowledge of good and evil. When you do, you will surely die."

Genesis 3:1–17

Adam turned over his dominion or authority to the devil. Adam's sin was high treason. God had given everything to Adam.

So he could rule this world with love—and Adam turned it all over to Satan.

The result of man's sin is an entrance into a spiritual death. Spiritual death separates us from God and unites with Satan.

> *"Wherefore, as by one man sin entered into the world, and death by sin; and so death passed upon all men, for that all have sinned."*
>
> (Romans 5:12 KJV)

Spiritual death

God is a spirit.

"God is a Spirit: and they that worship him must worship in spirit and in truth."

(John 4:24 NIV)

Satan is a spirit.

"For we wrestle not against flesh and blood, but against principalities, against powers, against the rulers of the darkness of this world, against spiritual wickedness in high places."

(Ephesians 6:12 KJV)

Man is a spirit.

"And the very God of peace sanctify you wholly; and I pray God your whole spirit and soul and body be preserved blameless unto the coming of our Lord Jesus Christ."

(1 Thessalonians 5:23 KJV)

God is a spirit and His nature is Life.

"For as the Father hath life in himself; so hath he given to the Son to have life in himself."

(John 5:26 KJV)

Satan is a spirit and his nature is death. (Read Ephesians 2:1–5.)

"Now the LORD God had planted a garden in the east, in Eden; and there he put the man he had formed. The LORD God made all kinds of trees grow out of the ground—trees that were pleasing to the eye and good for

food. In the middle of the garden were the tree of life and the tree of the knowledge of good and evil."

"A river watering the garden flowed from Eden; from there it was separated into four headwaters. The name of the first is the Pishon; it winds through the entire land of Havilah, where there is gold. (The gold of that land is good; aromatic resin and onyx are also there.) The name of the second river is the Gihon; it winds through the entire land of Cush. The name of the third river is the Tigris; it runs along the east side of Ashur. And the fourth river is the Euphrates."

"The LORD God took the man and put him in the Garden of Eden to work it and take care of it. And the LORD God commanded the man, "You are free to eat from any tree in the garden; but you must not eat from the tree of the knowledge of good and evil, for when you eat from it you will certainly die."

(Genesis 2:9, 16, 17 NIV)

Man ate, and he died. He was united with God, but now his spirit is united with Satan—which means death. Adam died spiritually, and then his body became death-doomed or mortal. He died physically some nine hundred years later.

"For if, by the trespass of the one man, death reigned through that one man, how much more will those who receive God's abundant provision of grace and of the gift of righteousness reign in life through the one man, Jesus Christ!"

"Consequently, just as one trespass resulted in condemnation for all people, so also one righteous act resulted in justification and life for all people. For just as through the disobedience of the one man the many were made sinners, so also through the obedience of the one man the many will be made righteous."

(Romans 5:17-19 NIV)

How can we prevent a spiritual separation from God from occurring? Take time to accept God into your life, study pray and invite God into your daily life. By doing this He becomes the cornerstone that supports every part of your life.

Chapter 13

The Holy Spirit

"Jesus, when he was baptized, went up directly from the water: and behold, the heavens were opened to him. He saw the Spirit of God descending as a dove, and coming on him. Behold, a voice out of the heavens said, "This is my beloved Son, with whom I am well pleased."

(Matthew 3:16–17 NIV)

At Jesus' baptism, the voice of the Father spoke out of the heavens, "This is my beloved Son," and the Spirit descended visibly upon Him in the form of a dove.

The people that witnessed Jesus' baptism heard the voice and saw the dove and also could have touched Jesus because Jesus was in their midst.

"But the Counselor, the Holy Spirit, whom the Father will send in my name, he will teach you all things, and will remind you of all that I said to you."

(John 14:26 NIV)

God is manifest in absolute Trinity: He is three in one. The three—Father, Son, and Holy Spirit—are absolutely one. Each Person is represented as God. That does not mean that each one is a part of God, but each one *is* God. Each one is the whole of God—God's personality is not divisible. God cannot be divided. The Father is first, the Son is second, and the Holy Spirit is third. One is not greater than the other.

When Christ came to earth as a man, He had a ministry to fulfill, and when He had accomplished it, He returned to the Father. He accomplished what He was sent here to do. His ministry had a time limit also, so in His appointed time, at Pentecost, the Holy Spirit came into the world having a definite mission to fulfill. His ministry is being carried on now in us and through us and will continue until completed, when at the appointed time we will ascend into heaven.

There has not been a revelation of the Holy Spirit in the physical sense like there was of Christ; however, there has been a revelation in believers in the physical sense. *Juanita asked God for His Holy Spirit with the overflow of speaking in tongues. She noted,* "He quickly gave me this gift with a heavy, electrifying anointing, and to me this was a real sense that God's Holy Spirit had been poured out on me. However, even if I had not received this physical sense or feeling, I would have believed and accepted it because God's Word says so. The Holy Spirit came to impart the nature of God to the Spirit of man, and His ministry could not be localized. He came to dwell in the bodies of those who had become a new creation in Christ.

> *"And I will ask the Father, and he will give you another advocate to help you and be with you forever—the Spirit of truth. The world cannot accept him, because it neither sees him nor knows him. But you know him, for he lives with you and will be in you.*
>
> (John 14:16, 17 NIV)

The Holy Spirit

When the Advocate comes, whom I will send to you from the Father—the Spirit of truth who goes out from the Father—he will testify about me. And you also must testify, for you have been with me from the beginning."

(John 15:26, 27 NIV)

"But very truly I tell you, it is for your good that I am going away. Unless I go away, the Advocate will not come to you; but if I go, I will send him to you."

(John 16:7 NIV)

The Holy Spirit had been the divine agent in creation so that our souls could complete the external destination that they were designed for—heaven—and so that they could be with our Lord and Savior. With the guidance of the Holy Spirit we will complete the race that has been laid before us.

Christ had to die for man's offenses, rise when man had been declared righteous, and enter into the Holy of Holies. With His own blood, He had obtained eternal redemption for man. When Jesus had done this He was glorified and sat down at the right hand of God. The Holy Spirit could be given—he came to impart the nature of God to the spirit of man in the new birth and then fill this new creature with the fullness of God.

At the time Jesus was alive the disciples and others that followed Jesus were under the old covenant. They did not understand the death or resurrection of Christ. The Holy Spirit was not given until Pentecost to reveal these truths and impart God's nature to man.

Jesus said these words:

"For John baptized with water, but in a few days you will be baptized with the Holy Spirit."

(Acts 1:5 NIV)

"I baptize you with water for repentance. But after me comes one who is more powerful than I, whose sandals I am not worthy to carry. He will baptize you with the Holy Spirit and fire."

(Matthew 3:11 NIV)

"For we were all baptized by one Spirit so as to form one body—whether Jews or Gentiles, slave or free—and we were all given the one Spirit to drink."

(1 Corinthians 12:13 NIV)

"For all of you who were baptized into Christ have clothed yourselves with Christ. There is neither Jew nor Gentile, neither slave nor free, nor is there male and female, for you are all one in Christ Jesus. If you belong to Christ, then you are Abraham's seed, and heirs according to the promise."

(Galatians 3:25-29 NIV)

Once you become a Christian you become an heir to the kingdom of God. That means our heavenly Father will take care of all His children, even His adopted children.

"John answered them all, "I baptize you with water. But one who is more powerful than I will come, the straps of whose sandals I am not worthy to untie. He will baptize you with the Holy Spirit and fire."

(Luke 3:16 NIV)

Step out in faith and immerse your very being into receiving the Holy Spirit, so you can walk as Jesus did.

The Holy Spirit

Being buried with Christ in water is typical of our burial with Christ in His death whereby the old man was crucified and put off. Being raised out of the water is typical of our resurrection with Christ out of spiritual death into eternal life, that we might walk in the newness of life.

My baptism is external, physical—it is just a type of what He does in the spirit of man. But He will immerse my spirit in the Holy Spirit and out of that immersion will come the new birth, and man will begin a new life.

> *"For we were all baptized by one Spirit so as to form one body—whether Jews or Gentiles, slave or free—and we were all given the one Spirit to drink."*
>
> (1 Corinthians 12:13 NIV)

This means the baptism into the Body of Christ is the birth into the Body of Christ; these Christians were immersed or baptized with the Holy Spirit.

> *"Don't you know that you are a temple of God, and that God's Spirit lives in you?"*
>
> (1 Corinthians 3:16 KJV)

> *"They were all filled with the Holy Spirit, and began to speak with other languages, as the Spirit gave them the ability to speak."*
>
> (Acts 2:4 WEB)

We receive by faith after we have asked for Him. God is no respecter of person. He gives to those who thirst and hunger and ask.

The evidence is the Word of God. But if the tongues were for the disciples, I wanted them too. I asked one day, and by faith I opened my mouth to praise God and suddenly started to praise my Lord in song in a heavenly language I did not know. God poured out His Spirit on me—through me—He bathed me, immersed me, in His liquid love. Each day I come to the throne for a refilling because as we give it out to others, we must be refilled.

Praise God. Hallelujah! Amen.

The Holy Spirit makes Jesus' walk on this earth a real event. He reproves the world of sin and leads us into right standing with God the Father. We are the instruments that the Holy Spirit uses to share the good news with the world.

The body of Christ is the church, and the church needs to be filled with the Holy Spirit so He can work freely through us.

> "No one has ever seen God; but if we love one another, God lives in us and his love is made complete in us."
>
> (1 John 4:12 NIV)

God abides in us through the Holy Spirit; His love is perfected in us. The word translates *perfected* in the Authorized Version means "complete." The thought is that if God dwells in us, His love can be completed through our lives. *It seems like so many people are broken and not a complete person. I feel a little broken sometimes but when I meditate on Him all the pieces of my spiritual man seem to come together.*

The Holy Spirit reveals the Christ who has conquered death, the grave, and hell and has been given a name above every other name—that part that could not be disclosed to the senses of man.

Chapter 14

Vacation to Israel

Juanita and Dudley took to a vacation to Israel in 1984. My wife Patti just recently uncovered a diary in our attic while she was cleaning and was discarding things we can't continue to store. One of the most valuable things that were left to us was all of Juanita's notes and journals.

Juanita's life was a great testament of who she was and how she wanted to live. She gave most of her money to her church and so many others that were in need.

This chapter about her vacation to Israel continues to let those reading this book know what kind of person she was and how she just wanted to have a close walk with God.

Tuesday, November 13, 1984

Slept good, with the Lord's help, despite the fact I knew I was on a plane one city block long carrying 494 people. We had a delicious dinner at midnight and a delicious breakfast two hours before we landed.

When Dud and I both saw Tel Aviv in the land of our Lord, we both broke into tears.

It took quite some time getting our luggage, finding our buses, and arriving at our Hilton hotel. We are in Room 1444 and on the Mediterranean Sea. Though it is nighttime already and we can hardly see the ships, they are visible. No street lights—this looks funny to us. Many buildings show the remains of some of the wars of the past. We praise God for a safe trip, for a wonderful bed and room, and the things that our Heavenly Father is already revealing to us. We want to be open to His revelation knowledge and to His sweet Holy Spirit.

We have met the Rennes from Iowa. We had a delicious dinner all served in courses, and it ended with ice cream, molded, with a thin cake on the bottom.

There are 294 people on our tour from all over the world, and God is so good to us to have allowed us to come to such a marvelous place.

Wednesday, November 14, 1984

We spent the night in Tel Aviv, a city of one million.

Rose early, dressed, went to breakfast, and then boarded the bus at 8:00 a.m. Our group from Agape is together on one bus. [Agape was her church in Little Rock.] We first went to Joppa, where Peter was told by the Lord to go to Caesarea, which is really a part of Tel Aviv. We are getting to see many ruins of ancient Joppa, and later we went to Haifa, a city set on a hill—many apartment houses, all built on the hill. We saw many ships, loading and unloading.

Went to Megiddo in the valley of Megiddo, where the first battle of the world was fought and where the last battle, Armageddon, will be fought. Our guide told us there was already an underground air base prepared for this battle.

Vacation to Israel

We saw the ancient city of Megiddo and walked down to see the water tunnel, which the king devised for his people so that when they were under attack they would have water.

We saw Caesarea, a Roman city, where Peter went and gave the first Gentiles the good news of Jesus.

The Mediterranean Sea was where Jonah ended up in the belly of the whale, and our hotel was directly on the Mediterranean Sea. We heard the water lapping all night.

There are four and a half million people in Israel in 1984—one million Arabs and three and a half million Jews.

We saw many orange groves and banana groves. Every inch of ground is planted and utilized by the Israelis. Their fruit and vegetables are truly blessed of the Lord. I have never eaten such delicious food.

We also saw many cotton fields that had been harvested. She noted that a man from Arkansas had brought cotton over and showed the Israelis how to plant and harvest. They had the cotton still in large blocks (loose) covered with plastic.

We stopped at the amphitheater where the emperor viewed the gladiators and dancers—the same amphitheater where Peter came and preached to the Romans.

The amphitheater is built on the sea, and the cold breezes cooled King Herod as he sat with 20,000 watching the gladiators and many Christians martyred by the lions.

King Herod the Great also built the Hippodrome for horse racing.

The Romans at that time were a pleasure-seeking group of people, seeking everything but God. This is the pagan city at the time of Peter, who brought the good news of Jesus, which turned the city upside-down for God.

Today there are many rich people who live high in the hills. We saw some of their homes and by our standards they were fifty- to sixty-thousand-dollar homes where we live, and they paid half a million or more for them here.

We saw many army vehicles and bases today. We saw soldiers at almost every bus stop out in the countryside.

Cars were from everywhere. Japanese or small European cars cost fourteen thousand American dollars, and gas was $2.40 per gallon.

The Hebrew language has been dead for 2,000 years, but is now being revived.

We saw Mount Tabor, the Mount of Transfiguration. This is also the mountain on which Deborah and the army chief conquered their enemies.

Nazareth. Our last stop is high in the hills. We went to the well where Mary received the message from Gabriel that she was chosen of God to bear His only Son. It was really too commercialized.

But Nazareth truly is a city built on a rock. The word *Nazareth* means "beginning of a branch," and that is what Jesus is: the branch from God to connect men and God.

There are still many small carpenter shops in Nazareth.

The road to Nazareth is truly a cut-back, hilly road—God provided a very trustworthy bus driver.

Haifa, the third largest city of Israel, is on Mount Carmel.

Saul and His sons were defeated on Mt. Gilboa.

We saw Cana, where Jesus performed His first miracle.

Thursday, November 15, 1984

Breakfast was good: a variety of cheeses, cereal, and raw fish (I didn't even touch this, but Dud loved it).

We immediately boarded a boat (large double-decker) to ride the Sea of Galilee. This was my highlight of the trip thus far. As we rode the calm sea—this was where Jesus walked on the water and where Jesus calmed the wind and the water—our two big boats stopped in the middle of the sea and one of the pastors held a preaching and worship service. Many of us were weeping, when we realized we actually were on the same water Jesus had been on many times and that His ministry was around both sides of the Sea of Galilee.

We then drove to the Mount of Beatitudes, where Jesus seated the people on the hillside in amphitheater fashion and taught them. His voice was carried in amplifier fashion from the wind of the sea. This was where He fed the five thousand on five loaves and two fishes. There are now churches on top of the mountain, but the hillside remains the same.

We drove to the site of the 1967 war, the Six-Day War—then again in 1973 (Three-Day War). The Syrians were trying to capture the water supply of Israel, which would be disastrous to Israel.

God miraculously enabled His Israeli army to defeat the Syrians by making one tank with one man sound like an army encamped on the hills around them. As I stood looking at the trucks in ruins—the mine field is still there and our guide led us through the mine field—I knew we served an almighty God who has a covenant with His children, the Israelis.

We went to Capernaum and saw the ruins of the synagogue where Jesus taught and the outline of Peter's house. We saw many small farms. We saw the farmers living in a small community with their farmland in the countryside.

We again saw groves of bananas, avocado groves, and orange groves. We drove past the Hot Spring of Tiberius.

Our group drove to the Jordan River and witnessed a beautiful baptismal service.

Many of the women had bought white robes to be baptized in. Truly we felt the presence of the Lord.

Our guide Nathan is a Jew—thirty-five years old and a bachelor. He had to go for two years to school at the university, then serve a year, and then pass an exam to be a licensed guide.

God has blessed all 294 of us on this trip.

Vacation to Israel

We leave tomorrow for Jerusalem.

Friday, November 16, 1984

We arose early after a blessed night's sleep, ready to go out and look at the Sea of Galilee again.

Dudley and I had a great breakfast: fresh fruit—dates, apples, and oranges—nuts, cheeses of all kinds, and several different kinds of Israeli bread. Dudley skipped the raw fish today. I would have skipped the raw fish, too.

Around 8:15 we left our hotel with our baggage and started traveling to Jerusalem, where we will spend the remainder of our trip.

We traveled though the Jordan Valley, seeing every inch being used for farming. There are two different kinds of farming-family life.

The kibbutz is where families live together in a commune-type life, and the children are raised by a nurse. The family spends three hours a day with the children. The children are well-educated and protected. The family works the farms.

The second type of farmer is the moshan. They live in individual houses or in an apartment house in a small group and travel to the acreage from the houses to farm, each having five to fifteen acres.

They grow lush vegetables and fruit—God has blessed them. The desert has truly blossomed like the rose of Sharon for these folks.

The Israelis do not go to bed hungry, and everyone has plenty to eat. They work and provide for themselves. God has blessed them.

We traveled the desert area where the Israelis wandered in the desert for forty years—the wilderness.

Jericho was the area where Joshua and Caleb came back with the report that it is a land of milk and honey. Jericho was where Zaccheus, the little man, crawled up in a tree to see Jesus.

Jesus walked this route many times and healed the sick, cast out devils, and preached the gospel.

Our highway was only a quarter mile from the Jordanian border. We saw the Israeli troops guarding the border all the way down the Jordan valley. We could see on the other side of the Jordan the Jordanian army, their guns and cannons, and their encampment.

In Jericho and all along the valley we saw the empty mud huts used to house Arab refugees from the 1948 war. Jericho is the city where Joshua went and had his men march around it seven times and the walls fell.

All the way to Jerusalem we saw many soldiers and jeeps, trucks and tanks. The Israelis are still fighting for their promised land.

We saw tribes of nomads, which are present-day shepherds, and a lot of sheep were on the hills.

Bethany is the town where Lazarus was raised from the dead. We visited his tomb. The Arab children were begging for money.

Vacation to Israel

Jerusalem, the city of peace—it looks like all the pictures I've ever seen. Houses, and even apartment houses, are built like the original house of limestone. They were one right after another on the hillside.

We saw the eastern gate through which Jesus will return.

We visited the Garden of Gethsemane. The same olive tree is there and the same oak Jesus knelt on and agonized.

We went into the Upper Room. This was the highlight of my day. It was the place where Jesus and His disciples ate the Last Supper together. It was also the place where the 120 on the Day of Pentecost received the baptism of the Holy Ghost—there was the power of God in this place. We saw the Mount of Olives where Jesus will return and it will be split wide open.

We visited the courtyard of Caiaphas's palace where Jesus was tried and scourged. We visited the pit where Jesus was kept until morning when he was crucified.

We saw the place where Jesus was denied by Peter three times.

At all these places there was a church built over them. We had a Christian guide from Detroit who worked for the united Christian embassy. He was in Israel hired by them to help with this Christian celebration of the Feast of the Tabernacle.

We visited Mount Mariah, where Moses offered up Isaac as a sacrifice.

We ate lunch in Jerusalem, supper in Bethlehem.

Juanita's Gift

Our hotel is tall. We are on the twentieth floor. Directly below us on the street across from us is the largest army compound we have seen. The soldiers are on every corner and every bus stop in the countryside. If only the Israelis could know that peace, true peace, has already come—Jesus.

We encountered a pickpocket going into the Upper Room. He was a little boy. He took one of the men's nice ballpoint pens. He got it away from him, however.

All in all, we have had a very blessed day—well-protected, delivered, and joyous.

Saturday, November 17, 1984

Our breakfast was delicious, as only the Israelis can cook and serve it—all kinds of bread and pastries, luscious fruit—and the usual raw fish (which I avoid like the plague).

Rain started about the time we went down for breakfast, so we pulled out all the rain gear—coats, etc. The Arab peddlers made a mint today selling umbrellas.

Since it is Shabbat (Jewish Sabbath), the stores are closed and traffic has stopped. Of course the Arabs go on as usual.

We saw many Jews going to the synagogue, all dressed in the Sabbath clothes. We noticed only the men and little boys going, so we questioned our guide. He said only the men and boys went to the synagogue; the women and girls stayed home. They cannot drive on the Sabbath and could only walk, not over a mile—so there are synagogues all over.

Vacation to Israel

We started out by driving the road Abraham took when God called Him out of Haran to the Promised Land. We went to the dome church where the huge rock Isaac was laid on (this was on top of Mount Moriah) to be sacrificed. You could go in only if you took your shoes off and left all of your belongings outside.

The ceiling was pure gold.

We saw the Hebrew university campus and drove up Mount Scopus. We stayed on the bus since it was raining so hard.

We visited the Mount of Olives and looked down on Jerusalem. We then drove down and began our trek through old Jerusalem, which is inside the Wailing Wall. Many of the things are from Jesus' time or at least a part of the floor or ceiling.

The highlight today was our visit to the stable where Jesus was born, which really was a cave underneath the inn. Today it was cold and damp, and I thought of our Lord.

Coming forth in such a place, I wept and wept as we began to sing, "O come let us adore Him"

The scary part of today was when our group nearly got separated in the narrow streets in the business part of old Jerusalem. The Arabs' businesses were open and the streets were so crowded with Jews and Arabs that it was a mass of people. I thought of the woman healed of the issue of blood and how as Jesus was going through the press she reached out and touched Him. Perhaps this was the same area. There were many, many different kinds of shops.

The Wailing Wall is made up of stones, some weighing three hundred tons.

We went to the area where Ruth met Boaz and where Boaz's workers gleaned the wheat.

We visited the shepherd's grove.

The World Leadership Conference started tonight. Of course part of the trip was to attend this. Our pastor preached the first sermon, which was on "taking your city for the Lord." There are many pastors and their wives on this trip.

All in all, today was a blessed day. Jerusalem got rain, which they needed badly, and He protected us and kept us dry.

Our bus driver is really directed of God. I am amazed at how he can handle a bus carrying sixty people on the very narrow roads.

Sunday, November 18, 1984

Today has been a glorious Lord's Day. We started out by waking early to a city socked by fog. Being on the twentieth floor of the hotel gave us a new experience in the fog—it was glorious.

We ate our now-traditional Israeli breakfast: all kinds of cheese, luscious fruit rolls, juice, and coffee. We also had tomatoes, cucumbers, radishes, and yogurt. Porridge was served for the cereal.

As we left the hotel, the taxi drivers were striking today and had the entire main road blocked. So to get to our destination, we had to take the back roads across the mountains to the Mediterranean Sea.

Vacation to Israel

We passed through Judah, a small town where John the Baptist was born. I learned something new today: the locusts John ate were long pods of chocolate carob—our guide climbed the tree and got us all a sample.

The mountain we were traveling on was the mountain where Samson met Delilah. We visited Ashkelon (the old and the new) right on the sea and we saw pillars from the temple like the ones Samson pushed down.

This was also one of the sites where David chose his five stones to slay the giant Goliath. We saw the mountain the Philistines were on, the mountain the Israelis were on, and David *did* kill the giant.

We saw Beth Shemesh, the place where the wagon carrying the ark stopped and the people came out to look at the ark and were killed.

There were beautiful avocado and olive orchards and vineyards.

We traveled back to Jerusalem on the Roman road from the sea. There were mile markers—Jesus said go not one mile but go two—these markers were what He was referring to.

We saw buses of school children viewing the countryside. This was a school day for them. There is a law saying the children must spend seven days a year seeing their country and learning about it.

We visited the city of Bedradim, a city of four thousand caves, all man-made, where people would dig the soft limestone out of the cave.

We visited Gath, the city of Goliath.

We visited Ashdod, a coastal city of 50,000.

The highlight of the day was visiting kibbutz-farm families working the land, living together and working together.

A severe battle took place here in 1967 when the Egyptians came to the coast going to Tel Aviv to capture Tel Aviv. They started firing on the farmers, who by the help of the Lord held them off.

We saw busload after busload of soldiers, many here at the Kibbutz as we listened to the recording about the 1967 war. I began to cry, for we in America are so blessed. Israel also is so blessed, but they have to repeatedly defend or possess their land. God's timing is about here. We are all feeling it as we walk among the people here and as we view the countryside. God will not be mocked.

Our meeting tonight of the World Leadership Conference was a blessed meeting of God.

Monday, November 19, 1984

I awoke early and meditated on what the Lord has been teaching me about Israel. Dressed and went down to our now very much traditional Israeli breakfast: cheese, fruit, special breads, juice, coffee—and raw fish (I'm still avoiding this as I would a plague).

We went first to the Garden Tomb—we went down into the empty tomb where Jesus arose. We toured the gardens here and had very special intercessory prayers for our church members and others.

We also viewed Golgotha, the place of Jesus' crucifixion.

The highlight of today was the Garden Tomb and our prayers.

Vacation to Israel

We then visited the Hadassah Medical Center complex, built and supported by the women of the United States (Zionist is Jewish.) We viewed the synagogue here with its glorious stained glass windows. Three were shattered not too many months ago by a bomb. They have been replaced and are covered in bulletproof glass. We drove past the Kennedy memorial.

Yad Vashim is a memorial to the Jewish Holocaust in Germany (we each had to have our handbag checked here) and what they [the Nazis] did to the world at that time. Seeing this was so very depressing, but it was a real experience. I came out crying because today in the United States we are murdering our little unborn children and using the protein of the fetuses in our collagen makeup. We as a nation need to repent to humble ourselves and pray for what we are doing.

The Holy land was so wonderful to see. We saw a huge model of the city of Jerusalem during the time of King David's period. Ein Karem was the place where John the Baptist was born. It looked very much like the place where Jesus was born.

Israel Museum was another highlight. Here we viewed the Dead Sea scrolls, the original scrolls of the Old Testament, and they could still be read. Our guide, a Jew, read to us out of the scroll of Isaiah.

We went to the Parliament building grounds and saw the huge menorah (seven candlesticks), which is the symbol of the country.

Our tour guide went to the university and studied the Bible and also how to be a guide.

Juanita's diary ended with this passage about the tour guide and the university.

What a wonderful vacation she and Dudley must have had. She praised God for everything about the vacation. It seemed she pretty much loved every part of the vacation—except for the raw fish for breakfast. She let her husband have every delightful bite.

Chapter 15

Get in Position to Receive

May 2, 1995

"The favor of God goes before me."

Jesus came into this world so that we might have life and enjoy it and have abundance.

Get out of survival mode. Get into a maximum mode, restoration is in the air.

Get in position to receive. Many Christians just exist and are not happy.

I'm going to enjoy life. That is my birthright because I'm a joint heir with Jesus! Amen!

Joy is like a morning espresso—don't leave home without it.

We need to keep the devil guessing.

I need to believe God for maximum results. When we believe in mankind more than we do God, we put limits on what God can do in our lives.

> *"That, however, is not the way of life you learned when you heard about Christ and were taught in him in accordance with the truth that is in Jesus. You were taught, with regard to your former way of life, to put off your old self, which is being corrupted by its deceitful desires; to be made new in the attitude of your minds; and to put on the new self, created to be like God in true righteousness and holiness."*
>
> *"Therefore each of you must put off falsehood and speak truthfully to your neighbor, for we are all members of one body. "In your anger do not sin." Do not let the sun go down while you are still angry, and do not give the devil a foothold. Anyone who has been stealing must steal no longer, but must work, doing something useful with their own hands, that they may have something to share with those in need."*
>
> *"Do not let any unwholesome talk come out of your mouths, but only what is helpful for building others up according to their needs, that it may benefit those who listen. And do not grieve the Holy Spirit of God, with whom you were sealed for the day of redemption. Get rid of all bitterness, rage and anger, brawling and slander, along with every form of malice. Be kind and compassionate to one another, forgiving each other, just as in Christ God forgave you."*
>
> (Ephesians 3:20–32 NIV)

Keep stretching for the knowledge of God and His abundance and you will find what you are looking for. Just remember: seek, and you will find.

Changing the way we think starts the process of changing who we are. It seems too easy to live an unwholesome lifestyle. I have had to make a lot of changes in how I think, so that I can get complete control of my life. I know I will be successful if I ask God for His help. Again, if you get control of your mind, you'll be able to control the rest of the things that have been controlling you. I've been struggling with trying to control my thoughts my entire life and will continue to ask for His help each day.

2 Corinthians 9:8

The nature of God is abundance. He performs miracles when there is lack and the only thing man can do is think about it.

I believe that you have to have a dream in your life, a vision of what you need or what you want to accomplish in life to move on to bigger and better things. I know that I have to fully trust in Him for all things and that His abundance and blessing will come.

I know that God wants to be part of our daily lives and wants to bless us by providing us with the desires of our heart. All you have to do is take a small step of faith and believe that He can be part of your life and then invite Him in.

My wife and I were having breakfast at Colonial Pancake House restaurant in Hot Springs Arkansas just recently and met a couple from Texas who loved to visit our great state. I told them about the book I was writing and told them that it was full of testimonies and that most of the testimonies were about God answering even the simplest of prayers. I told them I was going to send it to the publisher for the last round of editing and my new breakfast friend said she had a wonderful story that she would like to share. I told her I would love to put it in my book. She went on to say that it was just a simple request for something she needed.

"Story" by "Katheryn Bannon's

Has a cold, dreary, winter's day ever made you feel gloomy? Well, the weather has always had a direct effect on my mood. It was during a week-long ice storm that crippled all of north central Texas that I was at an all-time low. It had been an especially difficult year, including a failed business, illness, and a move across the country.

My husband and I were financially wiped out, and I was having difficulty recovering from a massive infection that had left me hospitalized for several days. The gloomy weather was more than I could take. I had felt distant from God for many months, and I began to pray for a restored relationship with Him. God was my only hope at this point in my life.

All I could think to do on this miserably cold day to improve my mood was read my Bible. That sounds simple enough. It was late in the evening, and reading my Bible was proving to be quite the challenge. I was just on the cusp of needing reading glasses at forty-six after twenty-one years of working behind a computer, but I was much too prideful to just buy a two-dollar pair, as though reading glasses would suddenly cast me into middle age. "I can still read fine," I would tell myself, "as long as I have plenty of light."

It was after dark before I could sit down to read as I babysat my one-year-old granddaughter, and she had other ideas that did not include me reading the Bible. I finally got her to sleep at about 9:00 p.m., and it was totally dark at this point. One would think that I could just sit by a lamp and begin reading, but not in my house because my husband insists on using low wattage bulbs in all of our lights—and I mean *all* of our lights. I was sitting as close to a lamp as possible with my arms as outstretched as they could be, and I could barely make out every other word I was reading. I was determined though.

God had put it in my heart to read my Bible right then, and I was going to read until I could read no more. I had been reading for about an hour when my daughter arrived to take my granddaughter home. She walked in, and we chatted for a minute before she reached into her coat pocket and tossed something in my direction. Lo and behold, it was a pair of reading glasses. She said that they were going to be thrown away at work, and she grabbed them out of the trash, thinking I could use them.

If that was not a clear sign from God to keep reading my Bible, I do not know what it is. It has been nine months since that cold, dreary night when God sent me a pair of reading glasses, and I have spent every spare moment reading my Bible and in prayer. The spiritual, emotional, and physical healing that has occurred in that time has been astounding, and it has all been because of our good Lord! I have learned to see God in all things, but especially the simple things—like a pair of two-dollar reading glasses. God is good all the time.

> *"I love those who love me, and those who seek me find me."*
> —Proverbs 8:17 (NIV)

Chapter 16

Amber's Story

July 26, 1986, started out as a typical summer day, with an appointment scheduled with our family's favorite eye doctor, Dr. Bill Simmons. Amber had been having some headaches and a lot of pressure during swimming lessons, so we thought she probably needed glasses. For a ten-year-old, she was pretty excited that she would soon be sporting a new fashion accessory, which was typical since she was about to head to middle school.

The appointment seemed to take a really long time since all the people in the waiting room emptied out. Since it was noon, no new patients were coming in. The nurse ushered me back to the examining area where Dr. Bill and his son, Dr. Rusty, were waiting with Amber. They reluctantly told me that Amber had papilledema, which meant a swollen optic nerve, and they wanted me to see an ophthalmologist in Little Rock, who was waiting for us.

It didn't dawn on me at the time that we could be facing something serious, and we had made plans to meet my mom and dad at Wendy's for lunch, so we headed there since I knew my parents would be waiting for us. However, my parents were alarmed, and we decided to go up to the doctor's office, calling my husband Terry to meet us there. Dr. George Schroeder examined Amber, scheduled a CAT scan, and gave us some options, all of which were not good, but I was clinging to the possibility of a pseudo brain tumor. He also mentioned that the MRI was new in Little Rock, and he wasn't sure insurance would pay for it. The procedure was expensive, but it would give a clearer picture. We assured him that we wanted it no matter what.

This all happened on a Friday; in fact, almost every test thus far happened on a Friday, which can be frustrating and scary because hardly anything gets done on the weekend. But I always looked at it as a time to get as much prayer going up as possible, and it always gave me peace. By Monday, the hospital had scheduled us an MRI, and by Tuesday, the neurosurgeon whom Dr. Schroeder recommended was calling us to tell us that the MRI showed a lesion and that he would meet with us on Wednesday. I honestly still did not know the seriousness of the situation we were facing.

On Wednesday, we met with Dr. Dickens, who gave it to us straight—a malignant brain tumor called an astrocytoma, which is usually not found in children, is a slow-growing tumor that can reoccur over time and could have been there all her life. It was at the back of her brain, which was operable. I remember hyperventilating, and he just kept giving me all this information, telling me that whether he told me or another doctor told me, it had to be dealt with. I asked what hope he could give, and he looked out the window and said, "There is so much technology and research being done these days." We called him Dr. Doom because he just seemed to talk and act without emotion, but we grew to love that man and realized that he was protecting his heart due to the nature of his occupation because he was a dad himself. He didn't usually operate on children. I was really seeing God's hand in every move we made.

We were scheduled to check into the hospital on Thursday, with surgery on Friday. Amber had been out in the waiting room with my parents while we talked to the doctor. On Wednesday afternoon, we had to break the news to her. She had been looking forward to going to church camp that next week, so just like a child, she couldn't begin to see the *big* picture; she just cried because she couldn't go to church camp. That night, she went up to Terry's parents' house to spend the night, and our house filled with friends from church. We formed a circle in the kitchen, and our pastor prayed that one day he would have a part in marrying Amber. We prayed for God's healing miracle for Amber.

On Thursday, we checked into the hospital. Thursday night, the community came together and prayed for Amber. We felt those prayers and heard so many wonderful stories of people coming back to the Lord who had been away, just to pray for Amber and get right with Him again.

Friday morning was the surgery, and the waiting room was packed! God was there and was taking care of every little detail, one of which was that I just didn't think I could see Dr. Dickens. He just spoke the truth, which I needed, but I didn't want to hear it. In walked Dr. Kuperman, my wonderful gynecologist who had delivered Amber! He found out about the situation and got permission to observe the surgery. He came into the waiting room and told me this. He was also going to be the one to come out when the surgery was over to tell me how it went. This was such divine intervention! Amber came through the surgery well. Dr. Dickens was aggressive with the tumor, and he felt he had removed all of it. The next few days would tell us if any of the areas of the brain that controlled gross motor function or anything else were affected.

In the next few days, finally out of ICU and back in the room, Amber appeared to be fine, except that she didn't seem to have emotions. She was pretty much "mono-emotion," with no expression of any kind. The doctor just said it was the trauma in her brain, and she would return, but it was very scary because she had been one happy little girl before the surgery. We did everything to bring her back too. Her room was filled with stuffed animals, flowers, and gifts from so many loving friends. My brother, his wife, and their daughter, who was very close to Amber, flew in. Amy piled up in the bed with Amber. A very good friend of ours who worked for us dressed up as a clown and brought so much cheer!

By the next Friday, with Amber's head wrapped in gauze, we begged the doctor to let us go home, and he told us that if we went straight home and rested, he would let us. We agreed, but as soon as we left, we took Amber and Amy to the movies to see *The Karate Kid*. They thought it was so cool to be so mischievous and sneaky! By now, we knew that life is short, and they would definitely not be doing anything wrong; we saw some of those smiles back!

In the months to come, we would take Amber to have radiation treatments at CARTI (Central Arkansas Radiation Therapy Institute), driving to Little Rock every day. We loved that place and those wonderful people who treat everyone, especially kids, like royalty! She would not get to start to middle school but would have to be homeschooled until treatments were finished. God, being there the whole time and always a few steps ahead of us, was planning a perfect homeschool teacher in our precious friend, Shirley Plant, who had just taken a leave from public school to focus on her own family. This was just a godsend because we all loved Shirley so much. Shirley loves the Lord, so we knew she was very comfortable with this plan.

When it was time for Amber to go to middle school, it was scary, since she was leaving the small community of Salem Elementary, where

Amber's Story

she had been all her life, to go to a huge setting where she hardly knew anyone. But once again, God was in control, putting her into a pod group of the most caring, loving teachers who made her feel so comfortable and loved. She adjusted very well to this new chapter in her life.

As time went by, MRIs were scheduled regularly. Each time, our family called on God for strength, peace, and healing. It was always a huge relief to hear or read "NED:" no evidence of disease! We could relax until the next MRI.

Life was beautiful! Our pastor, Bill Howard, who had prayed the night before the surgery that he would officiate Amber's marriage one day, had his prayer answered. In 1995, Amber married the man of all of our dreams, Shane Freeman, who had surrendered to the ministry and was serving as youth pastor at our church in the summer. He was going to go to Dallas Theological Seminary in the fall, and they would be living in Dallas, Texas.

In 1996, Amber and Shane came in for Thanksgiving, and we had her ten-year MRI scheduled that Wednesday night. We were all set to celebrate that we were free and clear of any cancer! Thanksgiving Day was full of family and food; on Friday, Amber and I headed out to do some shopping. When we walked in the door, the looks on Terry's and Shane's faces obviously showed that something was very wrong. Terry put his arms around me and said that Dr. Dickens had called. He saw something on the MRI. My legs literally went out from under me, but you know what? Immediately, I knew that this reoccurrence was for something much bigger than a tumor. I had this huge sense of peace that God really needed Amber and Shane to understand and grasp the power of healing that we, as her parents, knew from the experience ten years ago.

There was no better way for His glory to shine than for them, who were in the ministry now, to experience it as adults.

This time, the tumor was in the middle of her brain; it was very small but inoperable. Once again, God's omnipotence was so present when we found out that the gamma knife was now on the scene. It was a noninvasive way to zero in on the tumor and, with more radiation than she needed for a lifetime, zap the tumor. The surgery was set for December 18 in Dallas, Texas, where the neurosurgeon taking care of this "just happened" to be one of Dr. Dickens's professors in medical school. We knew we were continually in good hands! Right before the surgery, the doctors called us in to tell us that because they had to be aggressive with the radiation, we needed to understand that the brain cells that may be killed would never come back, and Amber might lose motor movement or other vital functions. The surgery would last twenty-two minutes, so we all went to different phones and started calling friends and relatives to get the word out. We didn't have social media at the time, so we had to rely on word of mouth and God. I called Salem Elementary, where I taught at the time, and they were happy to call a special meeting to the teachers' lounge, where my precious friends gathered and prayed fervently for a complete healing.

We had to wait six months for the gamma knife results, which again just gave us more time to draw close and pray for healing. Right before the appointment that would tell us the results, Terry was driving, praying, and thinking. He felt such a strong presence of God that he actually had to pull over because he felt like God was whispering to him, saying, "It's not there!" A sense of peace flooded Terry, and he held on to those words, not even sharing with anyone what he had experienced. The day we met with the doctor in Dallas, he walked into the room, turned to all of us, and said, "It's not there." We all fell apart, held hands, and cried

Amber's Story

and prayed, but later, when Terry shared his experience, we really fell apart. Also, Amber never experienced any loss of healthy brain cells, which was such a huge blessing.

There have been many more blessings than we could ever name here or, for that matter, in our whole life. Through it all, we loved the Lord and wanted to stay ever so close and praise Him for everything that happened, even if it wasn't what we desired for the moment. We knew that if it was His will, it would be the right thing, and we might or might not understand now or later.

Before Amber and Shane were married, we talked to them about the fact that Amber's first tumor was so close to her pituitary gland that she might not be able to get pregnant. Since Terry had a wonderful life story of being adopted into a beautiful home and becoming the amazing man that he is, Amber felt like she would probably be privileged to adopt too. But God had other plans and has blessed our family with two beautiful granddaughters. Amber has never forgotten how quickly life can change, and she compares little stresses in life to being in the hospital, which makes little stresses even smaller. She embraces every part of life as a gift and challenges people around her to do the same. She is a bright spot in the room and praises God for every day she has with her family!

Chapter 17

Fervent in Prayer

Fervency of Prayer in Your Life

Being passionate about your prayer life causes other people to desire the same open communication with Jesus that you have. So let others know about your prayer life and how it helps you through each day. Juanita lived this each and every day and she let the world know who she was as a Christian. I'm just treading water where Juanita was walking on the water.

One goal that I have is to be more like Him. Reading the Scripture below is telling us to confess to each other and I just did. Writing this book has been such a spiritual healing in my life.

Mark 4:19 teaches us to stay away from the things of the world that will ultimately cause us to stumble

> *But the worries of this life, the deceitfulness of wealth and the desires for other things come in and choke the word, making it unfruitful.*
>
> (NIV)

1. Cares of this world should not control us

2. Deceitfulness should not ever be part of who we are. Don't let greed rule or control who you are.
3. Lusts for things should not control us. *It's okay to have things but don't put them first in your life.*

> "Confess therefore your sins one to another, and pray one for another, that ye may be healed. The supplication of a righteous man availeth much in its working."
>
> (James 5:16 KJV)

Fervency is an intensity that is very hot and will be a burning enthusiasm for something.

We may exert a mighty force of passion to others, when we are walking in God's Spirit.

How do we know when we are not praying fervent prayer? You'll be excited about everything in life when you are. A wholesome prayer life will cause you to be passionate about your walk with God, and it will enhance all your relationships as well.

> *But it is always good to be zealous in a good cause, and not only when I am present with you. My little children, of whom I am again in travail until Christ is formed in you.*
>
> (Galatians 4:18–19 KJV)

Your fervent prayer will affect your spirit, soul, and body.

In Luke 22:44 Jesus was praying with every ounce of His very being for all of mankind.

Fervent in Prayer

Be fervent in the Spirit so you can grow in the Lord. It can be very hard to be excited about anything in life when life does not go the way it should. But when you add prayer, all things will change.

> *"Offer hospitality to one another without grumbling. Each of you should use whatever gift you have received to serve others, as faithful steward of God's grace in its various forms. If anyone speaks, they should do so as one who speaks the very words of God. If anyone serves, they should do so with the strength God provides, so that in all things God may be praised through Jesus Christ. To him be the glory and the power forever and ever. Amen."*
>
> (1 Peter 4:9–11 NIV)

We need to have a fervent love—enthusiastic love—for life and others.

How do I obtain the fervent prayer?

1. Ask God for what you need.
2. Stir yourself up and get moving in your walk with God

> *"Therefore, I urge you, brothers and sisters, in view of God's mercy, to offer your bodies as a living sacrifice, holy and pleasing to God—this is your true and proper worship."*
>
> (Romans 12:1 NIV)

"Story" By Chellie and Dale Longstreth

But As For Me and My House, We Will Serve The Lord.

My wife's good friend Rochelle was telling her that Rochelle's niece, Chellie, was looking for a house with her husband-to-be, Dale. They had made an offer on a house they thought was the one for them. The offer was accepted, but it later fell through.

They looked at several other houses, and nothing seemed right. Then they found another one. Their offer was accepted, but the process of purchasing the house just wasn't going smoothly, so they began to question if God even wanted them to have a house.

They both took a little time to pray about it and asked God to reassure them that they were doing the right thing. Rochelle, who likes to embroider, asked her niece what her favorite scripture was so that she could make a gift for the new house. Her niece answered, saying Joshua 24:15: "As for me and my house, we will serve the Lord." But before Rochelle started anything, Chellie wanted to ask Dale what he would like. Without hesitation he answered, "My favorite verse is 'As for me and my house, we will serve the Lord.'"

When they moved into the house and started to remodel, he found a framed picture hidden away in a basket under a table. That basket was covered with old silk flowers. The picture was a watercolor painting of the house made years ago, when it was first built. At the bottom of the painting was the scripture from Joshua 24:15: "As for me and my house, we will serve the Lord." There was their answer to prayer.

Sometimes we just get a reassurance in our spirit, and sometimes we get an answer written in His Word. God is amazing!

> "But as for me and my house, we will serve the Lord."
> —Joshua 24: 15 (KJV)

Chapter 18

No Poverty in Christ

"Story" by Russell Morrison

"The Lord is my shepherd, I shall not want."

—Psalms 23:1 (KJV)

"Therefore I tell you, do not worry about your life, what you will eat or drink; or about your body, what you will wear. Is not life more than food and the body more than clothes?"

—Matthew 6:31–33 (NIV)

*B*e generous with what we have and give to the poor. Let's bring them out of poverty by sharing Christ with them. When I was very young, my mother had to truly trust God just to put food on the table and I had wonderful friends that shared many a family meal to help me along.

I knew poverty well as a child. I grew up in a tough time and only knew financial and spiritual poverty until I found that I could rise up and out of what I was born in. Once I found the truth, I could actually remove myself from this ongoing inheritance of poverty. Believing and trusting has allowed me to walk out of the world of poverty and into the world of faith.

Poverty comes to seize control of our lives.
Poverty wants to rob us of everything we have and more.
Poverty will inhabit every part of your life if you let it.
Poverty will come in and occupy your home and job, and it will occupy all your thoughts.

Poverty begins as an attitude of the soul.

> *"The rich man's wealth is his strong city.*
> *The destruction of the poor is their poverty."*
> —Proverbs 10:15 (KJV)

The poor are destroyed.

> *"There is one who scatters, and increases yet more. There is one who withholds more than is appropriate, but gains poverty."*
> —Proverbs 11:24 (WEB)

Withholding is the badge of the poor. Give even when it hurts, and God will bless you.

> *"Whoever disregards discipline comes to poverty and shame, but whoever heeds correction is honored."*
> —Proverbs 13:18 (NIV)

> *"The love of sleep will bring poverty."*
> —Proverbs 20:13

Drunkards and gluttons will come to poverty.

Poverty can come in the form of lack, want, and destitution.

No Poverty in Christ

Jesus gave all of us the opportunity to claim the gift of eternal life by believing. He left all the riches in glory to become poor so that we could become rich in spirit, so don't you think it is time to make that claim of faith and enter into His presence?

> *"A little sleep, a little slumber, a little folding of the hands to sleep: so your poverty will come as a robber, and your scarcity as an armed man."*
> —Proverbs 6:10–11 (NIV)

> *"He becomes poor who works with a lazy hand, but the hand of the diligent brings wealth."*
> (Provebs 10:4 NIV)

I've been in the workforce for many years, and if you don't produce a good product, you will soon find yourself without a job.

> *"The hands of the diligent ones shall rule, but laziness ends in slave labor. Anxiety in a man's heart weighs it down, but a kind word makes it glad."*
> —Proverbs 12:24, 27 (WEB)

> *"Do you see a man skilled in his work? He will serve kings. He won't serve obscure men."*
> —Proverbs 22:29 (EST)

I've had the opportunity to work with a few great craftsmen like Bill Bown, who was one of those craftsmen who could just about build anything that you could imagine. He worked for some of the finest physicians in the Little Rock area, and I was fortunate to be taught the craft of cabinet building by him.

Be diligent in searching out the truth. Prosperity anointing comes when you get your soul in order.

"Beloved, I pray that you may prosper in all things and be healthy, even as your soul prospers. For I rejoiced greatly, when brothers came and testified about your truth, even as you walk in truth. I have no greater joy than this, to hear about my children walking in truth."

"Beloved, you do a faithful work in whatever you accomplish for those who are brothers and strangers."

—3 John 1:2–5 (WEB)

God's wish is that we prosper in Him. If you have a true spiritual walk with Him, you have already become rich beyond any material riches you may ever gain.

Chapter 19

There Are No Valleys in Jesus

Going through a valley? No, we don't have to go through the valley. Jesus has provided a way where we can walk in the glory of God.

When Adam and Eve were in the beautiful garden, there were no valleys—until they sinned. See, that is what Satan wanted for them: to be down and without—down in the valley. Before they sinned, they walked and talked with God in the cool of the day; fellowshipping met all of their needs.

Jesus will meet your every need, just trust him.

> *"And they heard the voice of the Lord God walking in the garden in the cool of the day, and Adam and his wife hid themselves from the presence of the Lord God amongst the trees of the garden."*
>
> (Gen 3:8 KJV)

Adam and Eve had been led astray, and they knew they were separated from God—now they were in the valley.

1. They were down and out

2. Afraid
3. Sorry for themselves
4. Blaming others. *It is so easy to blame others when you have made the wrong decisions in life. If you are having problems and blaming someone else for all the wrongs in your life, take a few minutes and ask God to open your eyes.*

God has provided for us a seat in the heavenly places so that we can have the spiritual blessings that we have inherited.

> *"Praise be to the God and Father of our Lord Jesus Christ, who has blessed us in the heavenly realms with every spiritual blessing in Christ. For he chose us in him before the creation of the world to be holy and blameless in his sight. In love he predestined us for adoption to sonship through Jesus Christ, in accordance with his pleasure and will—to the praise of his glorious grace, which he has freely given us in the One he loves. In him we have redemption through his blood, the forgiveness of sins, in accordance with the riches of God's grace that he lavished on us. With all wisdom and understanding, he made known to us the mystery of his will according to his good pleasure, which he purposed in Christ."*
>
> (Ephesians 1:3–9 NIV)

> *"As for you, you were dead in your transgressions and sins, in which you used to live when you followed the ways of this world and of the ruler of the kingdom of the air, the spirit who is now at work in those who are disobedient. All of us also lived among them at one time, gratifying the cravings of our flesh and following its desires and thoughts. Like the rest, we were by nature deserving of wrath. But because of his great love for us, God, who is rich in mercy, made us alive with Christ even when we were dead in transgressions—it is by grace you have been saved. And God raised us up with Christ and seated us with*

> *him in the heavenly realms in Christ Jesus, in order that in the coming ages he might show the incomparable riches of his grace, expressed in his kindness to us in Christ Jesus. For it is by grace you have been saved, through faith—and this is not from yourselves, it is the gift of God—not by works, so that no one can boast. For we are God's handiwork, created in Christ Jesus to do good works, which God prepared in advance for us to do."*
>
> (Ephesians 2:1–10 NIV)

We are the redeemed because of what Jesus did for us on the cross. We are blessed every day that we walk on this earth.

We should never have to go through another valley again. When we do happen to be in a valley, just put all your trust in Jesus. He will walk with you right out of those tough times into a victorious walk with Him into the light of His love.

> *"For he has rescued us from the dominion of darkness and brought us into the kingdom of the Son he loves, in whom we have redemption, the forgiveness of sins."*
>
> (Colossians 1:13, 14 NIV)

When we are in one of those valleys of life you need to make the decision to:

Leap over it with Jesus

1. Stay in the Word daily
2. Be obedient to the Word—when you pray, believe you receive and act like it.
3. Resist the devil—resist the devil and he will flee.

4. Cast down imaginations. Imagining things will completely take over all aspects of your life it you let it. *Don't waste your time on worrying about things that most likely will not happen.*

"Submit yourselves then to God. Resist the devil, and he will flee from you."

(James 4:7 NIV)

"We demolish arguments and every pretension that sets itself up against the knowledge of God, and we take captive every thought to make it obedient to Christ."

(2 Corinthians 10:5 NIV)

Get up every morning and begin to dance and praise God. Jesus is walking with us today. Ask the Holy Spirit for your assignment for the day.

How do we allow ourselves to get in the valley? When we take our eyes off of Jesus, things seem to fall apart. The Israelites were out in a harsh world and knew they had to keep their eyes on God, who was their only source. Imaginations can take over and control each and every one of our thoughts if we let them.

The idea is never take your eyes off the mark. If you want a peaceful life, keep pressing on with your eyes on Jesus.

Chapter 20

Healing

We are believers. As believers of God, we believe He is and that he created us. As believers, we need to keep on believing in Jesus, that He died for us, and that He will provide healing for us.

We are believers in His Holy Spirit who dwells in us. We are believers of His Word.

His word says, "By His stripes ye were healed." And again, "I am the Lord thy God that healeth thee."

He sent His word and healed them to heal us. Jesus manifested healing to the world.

If we are believers, why don't we receive? It is not God's fault. He has provided divine health for all of us.

Why we don't receive?

1. Faith in the Spiritual realm brings it to pass in the nature realm.

    If it's faith, then we need to get in His Word and study His Scriptures every day on healing. Confess these Scriptures.

2. Sin of strife—not walking in love

"Dear friends, if our hearts do not condemn us, we have confidence before God and receive from him anything we ask, because we keep his commands and do what pleases him. And this is his command: to believe in the name of his Son, Jesus Christ, and to love one another as he commanded us. The one who keeps God's commands lives in him, and he in them. And this is how we know that he lives in us: We know it by the Spirit he gave us."

(1 John 3:21–24 NIV)

"For where envying everything and strife is, there is confusion and every evil work."

(James 3:16 KJV)

There is no way that we can have faith to believe God for healing when we are striving or walking in strife—this is the arena for every evil work. Healing comes forth in the arena of faith and love, not in the arena of strife.

"For he that will love life and see good days let him refrain his tongue from evil and his lips that speak no guile."

(1 Peter 3:10 NIV)

Our confession should be the Word of God. What you put in will later come out come out.

"From now on, let no one cause me trouble, for I bear on my body the marks of Jesus."

(Galatians 6:17 NIV)

Think—meditate—on Him. This healing-Scripture needs to be in your heart.

Healing

We have not stood and believed in God for nothing. We need to continue to share His Word and believe in Him and to be faithful, and these things will follow us: peace, love joy, and the healing in our lives that we desire.

Resist the devil for symptoms of sickness like you resist him to sin.

One group teaches that God heals today in answer to special prayer or a special act of faith, according to His own will in the matter.

The second group teaches that healing for the body is the legal right of every child of God and that he receives healing for his physical body upon the same grounds that he receives remission of sin for his spirit.

An act of healing whereby God comes into immediate contact with man's physical body is no more a miracle than the new birth, in which God comes into immediate contact with the spirit of man, imparting to it His own nature.

Miracles are for today. God is still a miracle-working God. I've seen God perform miracles. *He has performed many miracles on me!*

If God heals only in an answer to a special act of faith and that only when He wills to, healing does not legally belong to the child of God and was not included in redemption.

But healing was a part of man's redemption in Christ. Healing belongs to every child of God, and no special act of faith is required to obtain it. There need be no questioning as to whether it is God's will to heal: if it is in the redemption, it is His will. Praise the Lord!

The origin of disease or sickness and death in man's physical body are but the manifestation of spiritual death within the spirit. If man had never died spiritually, disease and death would never have had a part in man's physical body.

Christ brought peace to the souls of men and healing to their bodies. Healing had a major place in the ministry of Christ.

Christ was the Father's will revealed to man, and He revealed that it was the Father's will to break the power of disease over man's body and set him free from pain and suffering.

> *"On a Sabbath Jesus was teaching in one of the synagogues, and a woman was there who had been crippled by a spirit for eighteen years. She was bent over and could not straighten up at all. When Jesus saw her, he called her forward and said to her, "Woman, you are set free from your infirmity." Then he put his hands on her, and immediately she straightened up and praised God.*
>
> *Indignant because Jesus had healed on the Sabbath, the synagogue leader said to the people, "There are six days for work. So come and be healed on those days, not on the Sabbath."*
>
> *The Lord answered him, "You hypocrites! Doesn't each of you on the Sabbath untie your ox or donkey from the stall and lead it out to give it water? Then should not this woman, a daughter of Abraham, whom Satan has kept bound for eighteen long years, be set free on the Sabbath day from what bound her?"*
>
> *When he said this, all his opponents were humiliated, but the people were delighted with all the wonderful things he was doing".*
>
> (Luke 13:10–17 NIV)

Christ clearly stated that Satan had bound this woman's physical body for eighteen years.

Healing

"A few days later, when Jesus again entered Capernaum, the people heard that he had come home. They gathered in such large numbers that there was no room left, not even outside the door, and he preached the word to them. Some men came, bringing to him a paralyzed man, carried by four of them. Since they could not get him to Jesus because of the crowd, they made an opening in the roof above Jesus by digging through it and then lowered the mat the man was lying on. When Jesus saw their faith, he said to the paralyzed man, "Son, your sins are forgiven."

"Now some teachers of the law were sitting there, thinking to themselves, "Why does this fellow talk like that? He's blaspheming! Who can forgive sins but God alone?"

"Immediately Jesus knew in his spirit that this was what they were thinking in their hearts, and he said to them, "Why are you thinking these things? Which is easier: to say to this paralyzed man, 'Your sins are forgiven,' or to say, 'Get up, take your mat and walk'? But I want you to know that the Son of Man has authority on earth to forgive sins." So he said to the man, "I tell you, get up, take your mat and go home." He got up, took his mat and walked out in full view of them all. This amazed everyone and they praised God, saying, "We have never seen anything like this!"

(Mark 2:1–12 NIV)

"Therefore, just as sin entered the world through one man, and death through sin, and in this way death came to all people, because all sinned—"

"To be sure, sin was in the world before the law was given, but sin is not charged against anyone's account where there is no law. Nevertheless, death reigned from the time of Adam to the time of Moses, even over those who did not sin by breaking a command, as did Adam, who is a pattern of the one to come."

"But the gift is not like the trespass. For if the many died by the trespass of the one man, how much more did God's grace and the gift that

came by the grace of the one man, Jesus Christ, overflow to the many! Nor can the gift of God be compared with the result of one man's sin: The judgment followed one sin and brought condemnation, but the gift followed many trespasses and brought justification. For if, by the trespass of the one man, death reigned through that one man, how much more will those who receive God's abundant provision of grace and of the gift of righteousness reign in life through the one man, Jesus Christ!"

"Consequently, just as one trespass resulted in condemnation for all people, so also one righteous act resulted in justification and life for all people. For just as through the disobedience of the one man the many were made sinners, so also through the obedience of the one man the many will be made righteous."

"The law was brought in so that the trespass might increase. But where sin increased, grace increased all the more, so that, just as sin reigned in death, so also grace might reign through righteousness to bring eternal life through Jesus Christ our Lord."

(Romans 5:12–21 NIV)

"Surely he took up our pain and bore our suffering, yet we considered him punished by God, stricken by him, and afflicted. But he was pierced for our transgressions, he was crushed for our iniquities; the punishment that brought us peace was on him, and by his wounds we are healed.

We all, like sheep, have gone astray, each of us has turned to our own way; and the LORD has laid on him the iniquity of us all."

(Isaiah 53:4–6 NIV)

Man's redemption from spiritual death is to be a complete redemption. It must be redemption from disease as well as sin. God realized this, and He has clearly shown us in His Word that He has made provision for the healing of man's body.

Healing

God laid all our sins and disease upon Jesus. He completely took them for all for us, praise the Lord!

Satan, who had the authority in the realm of spiritual death, has been brought to naught. Jesus won the victory in disease and sickness.

He has commissioned us to be His representatives to go out and share the gospel with others.

As Christians we are to lay hands on the sick so that they will recover. We are to do what Christ would have done if He were here in the flesh.

> *"And these signs will accompany those who believe: In my name they will drive out demons; they will speak in new tongues; they will pick up snakes with their hands; and when they drink deadly poison, it will not hurt them at all; they will place their hands on sick people, and they will get well."*
>
> (Mark 16:17, 18 NIV)

There are a few churches in the United States that handle snakes in the church services, I guess to prove that God will be provide them with safety while they worship. I don't think my faith is strong enough to pick up snakes, plus I think a have a little more common sense than to tempt my faith to do that.

Chapter 21

Wavering Faith

"But if any of you lacks wisdom, let him ask of God, who gives to all liberally and without reproach; and it will be given to him. But let him ask in faith, without any doubting, for he who doubts is like a wave of the sea, driven by the wind and tossed. For let that man not think that he will receive anything from the Lord. He is a double-minded man, unstable in all his ways."

(James 1:5–8 WEB)

What does anti-Christ mean? "False Christ," or a substitute for the real thing.

Think about it, who brings doubt into our lives? It's not God.

"Now the serpent was more subtle than any beast of the field which Jehovah God had made. And he said unto the woman, Yea, hath God said, Ye shall not eat of any tree of the garden?"

(Genesis 3:1 KJV)

"Every good gift and every perfect gift is from above, coming down from the Father of lights, with whom can be no variation, nor turning shadow."

(James 1:17 WEB)

God is not changeable. God is not intimidated. God does not have parallels.

God is absolute Truth. There are no variables in God. There is no degree of turning or wavering.

The world's system competes with God's truth every day. I'm supposed to have a one-track mind, and that should be the mind of Christ in me.

> "For I am the LORD, I change not; therefore ye sons of Jacob are not consumed."
>
> (Malachi 3:6 KJV)

Here the Word is telling us that God does not change.

> "Jesus Christ is the same yesterday, today, and forever."
>
> (Hebrews 13:8 KJV)

God does not alter His Word. God's Word has been tried.

Double-minded men and women stay confused about how they should worship God. They vacillate in opinion or don't have a purpose. We have to be able to decide who we are and not be indecisive in our beliefs and what we stand for.

Doubt: To withdraw from or to oppose and to act against.

> "They said to you that "In the last time there will be mockers, walking after their own ungodly lusts." These are they who cause divisions, and are sensual, not having the Spirit. But you, beloved, keep building up yourselves

on your most holy faith, praying in the Holy Spirit. Keep yourselves in God's love, looking for the mercy of our Lord Jesus Christ to eternal life."

(Jude 18:19 WEB)

The devil operates through the world system and controls people through the five senses.

"But let him ask in faith, without any doubting, for he who doubts is like a wave of the sea, driven by the wind and tossed."

(James 1:6 WEB)

The opposite of doubt is belief.

Wavering—it is so easy to waver and to want to go back and forth on who we are. But stay in the faith, and don't let the world change you.

Faith has resolution. My faith has to come from God's original faith to have a perfect resolution.

We must work on our personal faith. Faith has conviction. The devil tries to get us over in reasoning. We are to have no shadow of doubt.

True belief—God's children are not doubters. Go fellowship with the Father. Get around people or who have doubts.

I need a personal conviction. I must believe God for myself.

Fear is the father of all doubt.

How can we get rid of double-mindedness?

The devil will come at you in two different ways.

1. Internal strife in yourself. So don't struggle with things that are not true. If you are still struggling with something, you haven't heard from God.

2. Immutable things or things that are unchangeable.

The word of God can't be changed. God's character can't be changed. My character and God's character should be the same. God is more willing to see His promise come to life in our lives.

We need to be able to hear God's voice. Know your covenant rights in who you are as a Christian. Spend quality time with God so you will know His voice. Shed worldly thinking, and don't change horses in the middle of the stream. Work at developing your faith by trusting in God in every aspect of your life.

> So don't be anxious about tomorrow. God will take care of your tomorrow too. Live one day at a time.
>
> In Matthew 6:34 Jesus once told His disciples, "Seek ye first the kingdom of God, and his righteousness, and all these things shall be added unto you."
>
> *The "things" He spoke of, were the things that make us feel happy and secure—food, drink, clothes, and shelter. He told us not to make these the chief goal of our lives but to "seek the kingdom" and these needs would be automatically supplied. There, if we will take it, is the secret of happiness.*

Chapter 22

Linda's Story

At the end of December 2003, while coming home from the grocery store, I had a seizure, lost consciousness, and had a severe automobile accident. Amid a lot of confusion and disorientation, I heard men talking about amputating my legs to remove my body from the wreckage. At this time, I could see a hand reaching toward me and a voice saying, "It's not time." Suddenly all of my wits came to me, and I reached over and placed my hand upon one of the men's arm. I stated that I was a Christian and believed in God. I asked the men to please pray with me and seek God's will. I was freed from the car, placed in an ambulance, and transported to a helicopter. I was then flown to a trauma center hospital. At this time, I knew that my only hope was to rely on God to carry me through whatever I was going to face.

When I reached the ER, I learned that my right foot was severed above the ankle, my left foot was almost detached from my leg, and my right shoulder was dislocated. This whole ordeal seemed like a bad dream.

> *"The earnest prayer of a righteous person has great power and produces wonderful results."*
>
> —James 5:16

After seventeen surgeries within the first month, the doctors' hopes of me walking again were slim. I chose to try and keep my own feet (which were reconnected through the use of screws and metal rods, transplanted muscle from my back, and grafted skin from my thigh) instead of prosthetic feet. Again I trusted in the Lord and followed what I felt He had laid upon my heart to do for His glory.

Later I was asked if I was sure that the prayer and conversations had happened since I was seizing and really didn't know. I prayed that the Lord shine an answer down if this was His story. Months later, my aunt, who lived in my mother-in-law's quarters, had to be taken to the hospital by ambulance. The paramedic who came thought I looked familiar. When he got my aunt to the hospital, he came up to my sister and asked if I was who he thought. They started talking, and he told my sister the amazing story of the day that I asked for prayer and how things started turning around. Of course she called crying and telling me that my story was true and that I should shout it from the mountaintops.

After the outside rods were removed from my legs, my husband built rails in our hallway so that I could do rehabilitation and try to strengthen my legs. Every time I rolled my wheelchair up to the rails, I called upon the name of Jesus, for I knew that the footprints in the sand were His, and He would carry me.

After a series of tests, the doctors thought that my seizure was caused by stress. In January 2005, my son (who was eight years old) thought I was asleep, snoring on the couch. With his recorder in hand, he was going to catch me. When he entered the room, he noticed blood bubbles coming from my mouth and my body seizing. He threw his recorder in a panic, rushed over, and dumped the blood from my mouth; he then yelled for his brothers (fifteen and sixteen years old). One called 911 while the other tried to get my attention. During this time, our pastor showed up and was able to comfort my children. God was in control.

Once I was in the ER, the doctors discovered that I had broken my right hip. When they repaired my hip, the doctors ran more tests to explain the seizure. This time, they located on the MRI a tumor the size of a lime in my head. It was attached to the brain. When I thought I was crawling up from the valley, a landslide started again. I recall Psalm 23:2, which says, "He makes me lie down in green pastures; he leads me beside quiet waters."

I knew with Him by my side, I would fear no evil. With what I was facing, I knew that His words were where my comfort would come from.

My neurologist explained the complications I could face, the worst of which would be losing the ability of the right side of my brain. The tumor had to be removed. But I know an awesome God and knew at the time that His plan was in place, for my strength would come from Him.

> *"For I will restore health to you, and I will heal your wounds, says the Lord."*
>
> —Jeremiah 30:17

In ten years, I have had twenty-six surgeries. After every surgery, the Lord has seen to the success of my recovery. I use this testimony to comfort and give peace wherever He sends me.

"God is the potter, and I am His clay." I know that He is the author and finisher of my faith. I truly trusted in Him. It is up to God to mold, transform, and sanctify my journey through my earthly life. Amen.

Chapter 23

Be Perfect in God

Jesus said to us, "Be ye therefore perfect." Then He goes on to live a life of perfectness, doing His Father's will constantly and not yielding to Satan at any time.

He came to earth, hid His divinity, and had a flesh-and-blood body.

> *"Who, being in very nature God, did not consider equality with God something to be used to his own advantage; rather, he made himself nothing by taking the very nature of a servant, being made in human likeness. And being found in appearance as a man, he humbled himself by becoming obedient to death—even death on a cross!"*
>
> (Philippians 2:6–8 NIV)

He was tempted—but without sin. He showed to us how to have a perfect walk as humans in this world.

How should we walk? We should walk in the Spirit and not in the flesh. I can say this, but it has been very hard to do. This old guy has to ask for God's help with this one every day. We were transported from spiritual death to life by doing what

God wanted us to do. We seem to be absorbing everything that the world offers. Take time to absorb His Word. It will make a change in who you are in Christ.

> "For we do not have a high priest who is unable to empathize with our weaknesses, but we have one who has been tempted in every way, just as we are—yet he did not sin."
>
> (Hebrews 4:15 NIV)

He was tempted in all points for our sakes.

> "For it is God who works in you to will and to act in order to fulfill his good purpose.
>
> Therefore, my dear friends, as you have always obeyed—not only in my presence, but now much more in my absence—continue to work out your salvation with fear and trembling, for it is God who works in you to will and to act in order to fulfill his good purpose.
>
> Do everything without grumbling or arguing, so that you may become blameless and pure, "children of God without fault in a warped and crooked generation." Then you will shine among them like stars in the sky as you hold firmly to the word of life. And then I will be able to boast on the day of Christ that I did not run or labor in vain. But even if I am being poured out like a drink offering on the sacrifice and service coming from your faith, I am glad and rejoice with all of you."
>
> (Philippians 2:13–16 NIV)

He is at work in our lives, working out His good pleasure.

It seems that God is working in my life just about every day. When you read this Scripture, it is saying that God can't make changes in us until we stop complaining and griping about every little thing that irritates us. Once we change, we will be like shining stars in the sky and be like Him.

"Therefore, I urge you, brothers and sisters, in view of God's mercy, to offer your bodies as a living sacrifice, holy and pleasing to God—this is your true and proper worship. Do not conform to the pattern of this world, but be transformed by the renewing of your mind. Then you will be able to test and approve what God's will is—his good, pleasing and perfect will."

"For by the grace given me I say to every one of you: Do not think of yourself more highly than you ought, but rather think of yourself with sober judgment, in accordance with the faith God has distributed to each of you. For just as each of us has one body with many members, and these members do not all have the same function, so in Christ we, though many, form one body, and each member belongs to all the others. We have different gifts, according to the grace given to each of us. If your gift is prophesying, then prophesy in accordance with your faith; if it is serving, then serve; if it is teaching, then teach; if it is to encourage, then give encouragement; if it is giving, then give generously; if it is to lead, do it diligently; if it is to show mercy, do it cheerfully."

"Love must be sincere. Hate what is evil; cling to what is good. Be devoted to one another in love. Honor one another above yourselves. Never be lacking in zeal, but keep your spiritual fervor, serving the Lord. Be joyful in hope, patient in affliction, faithful in prayer. Share with the Lord's people who are in need. Practice hospitality."

"Bless those who persecute you; bless and do not curse. Rejoice with those who rejoice; mourn with those who mourn. Live in harmony with one another. Do not be proud, but be willing to associate with people of low position. Do not be conceited."

"Do not repay anyone evil for evil. Be careful to do what is right in the eyes of everyone. If it is possible, as far as it depends on you, live at peace with everyone. Do not take revenge, my dear friends, but leave room for God's wrath, for it is written: "It is mine to avenge; I will repay," says the Lord. On the contrary:

> *"If your enemy is hungry, feed him;*
> *if he is thirsty, give him something to drink.*
> *In doing this, you will heap burning coals on his head."*
> *"Do not be overcome by evil, but overcome evil with good."*
>
> (Romans 12:1–21 NIV)

Look at Jesus as our example of how to live the perfect life.

1. He walked a faith-walk—like we are to walk.
2. He needed food to feed the multitude—He took the food, blessed it, and God multiplied it.
3. He needed money to pay the taxes—Peter cast the net into the sea, and a fish he caught had the money in its mouth.
4. When He laid His hands on people, they were healed.
5. When He called Lazarus, Lazarus came forth and was raised from the dead.
6. He walked a love-walk.
7. He operated at all times in the love of His Father.
8. God's love was in Jesus, and God's love is in us.
   Jesus walked and operated in faith perfectly, and we should follow His example.

> *"I made known to them your name, and will make it known; that the love with which you loved me may be in them, and I in them."*
>
> (John 17:26 WEB)

Judge no man. Jesus loved, and he never judged any man. He loved so much that He walked the lonely road to the cross. He did those things that pleased the Father—as we are to do. He spoke only what the Father spoke.

Be Perfect in God

God is a faith God. God is a loving God. Jesus showed us perfect faith and perfect love. Jesus is our example. Perfect love—perfect love casts out fear. He never was offended nor offended anyone. He never presumed. He never presumed anything about anyone or wondered why, but instead He took them to the Lord.

He forgave the thieves, He forgave the soldier, and He forgave those that crucified Him.

Chapter 24

He Changed His Last Name

Thirty years after his mother's death, Rob Smith found an unusual way to honor her.

After more than four decades, Rob still feels a knot in his stomach when he thinks about his father. He didn't see him much after he was 5 years old.

Although his dad rarely called, Rob remembers his tearful, sobbing voice. "He would tell me how much he loved me and that he would come and see me sometime." He promised they'd go to ballgames together … spend some time camping … just the two of them.

But every promise proved empty.

His mother, Lucille Hernandez Smith, worked two or three jobs and spoke little about Rob's dad. He had to learn from his uncles that his father was an alcoholic who "drank away the paycheck."

Missing pieces
Rob missed having a dad "to take me camping, to teach me to drive, to come to my games, to teach me life." But his mother did her best to

fill the roles of both mom and dad. She taught her children right from wrong and how to care for those who had less. "There weren't that many who had less than us," Rob says.

Rob didn't make it easy for her. He recalls the day he and his mom dropped his high school girlfriend off at her house. After watching the girl walk alone across the street and up about 20 flights of stairs, Lucille asked, "Do you always drop her off like that?"

"Like what?"

Lucille told Rob that he should not only pick up his girlfriend at the front door, but also bring her back there … no matter how many steps he'd have to walk up.

Rob was annoyed. "This is why I need a father. Where is he? I should know these things and don't, so get off my back."

Lucille began to cry. "She also felt the missing pieces to our family," Rob says.

No place to call home
Life took a turn for the worse after Rob's senior year of high school. His mother just couldn't shake a bad summer cold, and when she finally went to the doctor she was diagnosed with cancer. A few months later, it got so bad that she couldn't work.

As Lucille lay on her deathbed at home, she begged Rob to read the Bible to her. Sometimes, after reading passage after passage, he would try to slip out of her room, thinking that she had drifted off to sleep. That's when he'd hear her say: "Keep reading—it's the words of God."

"It was in those moments of reading truth while she lay there dying," Rob says. "… [that] I found real life in Jesus."

Rob Smith was just 19 years old when his mother slipped into eternity. But because of his personal relationship with Jesus Christ, he wasn't alone.

A dream fulfilled
Now, after more than three decades, Rob continues to reflect on the positive impact of his mother's life. He's done his best to follow her example—to to point his children to faith in Christ.

He's also tried to give his children the things that he lacked growing up. "I strived to be the best dad," he said, "To give them academics, athletics, and confidence in Christ."

Despite this, he's continued to be haunted by the same questions: Why couldn't his legacy carry the name of the woman who pointed him to Christ and sacrificed so much for her children?

Why couldn't his family have a name that reflected their Hispanic heritage?

Then in the summer of 2013, his grown sons, Nate and Jake, had an answer: "Why couldn't the entire family change their last name—together?"

Rob mulled over their suggestion. Could his wife, Teresa, and their sons really change their last name from Smith to Hernandez?

He had long ago forgiven his father for deserting the family, so his purpose in doing this wouldn't be to dishonor him. And after all, his father had been dead for more than 20 years.

Then he began to wonder, *Why not follow through and become a Hernandez? Why not honor my Hispanic heritage and the mother I loved?*

The process wasn't easy. But after months of legal counsel and hard work, Rob and his wife, Teresa, and their two sons became the Hernandez family.

The old name Smith, with its reminder of Rob's broken past, is gone. And the new has come.

With the change of name, Rob threw down the gauntlet for Nate and Jake. It is now up to them to carry on the legacy that their grandmother once began: Hope in Christ. Commitment to family. Care for others.

Lucille's time on this earth is over. But the journey through life for the Rob Hernandez family has just begun.

Chapter 25

Fruit of the Spirit

The fruit of the spirit is our supernatural-natural disposition that prevents us from being selfishness, self-centered, and just sad without His love. Yield to the Holy Spirit each day so you can experience one of God's precious fruits, and that is love.

I must spend time with God.

"So I say, walk by the Spirit, and you will not gratify the desires of the flesh. For the flesh desires what is contrary to the Spirit and the Spirit what is contrary to the flesh. They are in conflict with each other, so that you are not to do whatever you want."

(Galatians 5:15, 16 KJV)

"We must sow to the spirit, and I must guard my heart. We must be diligent in keeping our hearts alive in Him."
"Above all else, guard your heart,
for everything you do flows from it."

(Proverbs 4:23 NIV)

We must keep the Word in our hearts to increase spiritually.

I want and must spend time in a living contact with God. The issues of life will not affect you when you are walking in the spirit.

Walking in love is not an option but a commandment. We must keep a living contact with the Father, which is prayer.

> *"But the fruit of the Spirit is love, joy, peace, forbearance, kindness, goodness, faithfulness, gentleness, and self-control. Against such things there is no law. Those who belong to Christ Jesus have crucified the flesh with its passions and desires. Since we live by the Spirit, let us keep in step with the Spirit."*
>
> (Galatians 5:22–25 NIV)

Walk in the fullness of God and you will walk in His love.

> *"Love is patient, love is kind. It does not envy, it does not boast, it is not proud. It does not dishonor others, it is not self-seeking, it is not easily angered, it keeps no record of wrongs. Love does not delight in evil but rejoices with the truth. It always protects, always trusts, always hopes, always perseveres."*
>
> *"Love never fails. But where there are prophecies, they will cease; where there are tongues, they will be stilled; where there is knowledge, it will pass away."*
>
> (1 Corinthians 13:4–8 NIV)

Love never fails. Love—agape love—wins the world to God.

Christ wants us to love one another. We do not want to turn anyone away by not loving them.

Fruit of the Spirit

> "As a prisoner for the Lord, then, I urge you to live a life worthy of the calling you have received. Be completely humble and gentle; be patient, bearing with one another in love."
>
> (Ephesians 4:1–2 NIV)

> "Wake up, sleeper, rise from the dead, and Christ will shine on you."
>
> Be very careful, then, how you live—not as unwise but as wise, making the most of every opportunity, because the days are evil. Therefore do not be foolish, but understand what the Lord's will is. Do not get drunk on wine, which leads to debauchery. Instead, be filled with the Spirit, speaking to one another with psalms, hymns, and songs from the Spirit. Sing and make music from your heart to the Lord, always giving thanks to God the Father for everything, in the name of our Lord Jesus Christ."
>
> (Ephesians 5:14–21 NIV)

The love of God takes care of divisions among people. One thing we all can agree on is love. Love makes allowances—be eager and strive to keep the harmony.

> "Instead, speaking the truth in love, we will grow to become in every respect the mature body of him who is the head, that is, Christ."
>
> (Ephesians 4:15 NIV)

When we walk in love, strife and confusion will not be present.

> "Love is patient, love is kind. It does not envy, it does not boast, it is not proud."
>
> (1 Corinthians 13:4 NIV)

Envy is our enemy, and it will kill, steal, and destroy us. Love never is envious, discontent, or possessing a feeling of ill will because of others' advantages, possessions, or success. We don't have to take a thought the enemy puts there. We fight the devil with the Word of God so we can overcome spiritual forces that come at us to destroy who we are in Christ.

> *"A heart at peace gives life to the body,*
> *but envy rots the bones."*
>
> (Proverbs 14:30 NIV)

Envy is a work of the flesh and not of the spirit.

> *"Furthermore, just as they did not think it worthwhile to retain the knowledge of God, so God gave them over to a depraved mind, so that they do what ought not to be done. They have become filled with every kind of wickedness, evil, greed and depravity. They are full of envy, murder, strife, deceit and malice. They are gossips, slanderers, God-haters, insolent, arrogant and boastful; they invent ways of doing evil; they disobey their parents."*
>
> (Roman 1:28–30 NIV)

> *"So I say, walk by the Spirit, and you will not gratify the desires of the flesh. For the flesh desires what is contrary to the Spirit, and the Spirit what is contrary to the flesh. They are in conflict with each other, so that you are not to do whatever you want. But if you are led by the Spirit, you are not under the law."*
>
> *"The acts of the flesh are obvious: sexual immorality, impurity and debauchery; idolatry and witchcraft; hatred, discord, jealousy, fits of rage, selfish ambition, dissensions, factions and envy; drunkenness, orgies, and the like. I warn you, as I did before, that those who live like this will not inherit the kingdom of God."*

"But the fruit of the Spirit is love, joy, peace, forbearance, kindness, goodness, faithfulness, gentleness and self-control. Against such things there is no law."

(Galatians 5:16–23 NIV)

Envy is darkness and of the devil.

"Furthermore, just as they did not think it worthwhile to retain the knowledge of God, so God gave them over to a depraved mind, so that they do what ought not to be done. They have become filled with every kind of wickedness, evil, greed and depravity. They are full of envy, murder, strife, deceit and malice. They are gossips, slanderers, God-haters, insolent, arrogant and boastful; they invent ways of doing evil; they disobey their parents; they have no understanding, no fidelity, no love, no mercy."

(Roman 1:28–31 NIV)

Always say you are glad they are being blessed, and don't be envious of what others have or who they are. You are a joint heir with Christ so chase after your blessing and not after others.

Chapter 26

Enemies of Love

The fruit of the spirit is the character of God.

"But whoso keepeth his word, in him verily is the love of God perfected."
(1 John 2:5 KJV)

Keep God's Word next to your heart and you will get closure to the heart of God.

"I am the true vine, and my Father is the gardener. He cuts off every branch in me that bears no fruit, while every branch that does bear fruit he prunes so that it will be even more fruitful. You are already clean because of the word I have spoken to you. Remain in me, as I also remain in you. No branch can bear fruit by itself; it must remain in the vine. Neither can you bear fruit unless you remain in me."
   "I am the vine; you are the branches. If you remain in me and I in you, you will bear much fruit; apart from me you can do nothing. If you do not remain in me, you are like a branch that is thrown away and withers; such branches are picked up, thrown into the fire and burned. If you remain in me and my words remain in you, ask whatever you wish, and it will be done for you. This is to my Father's glory, that you bear much fruit, showing yourselves to be my disciples."
(John 15:1 NIV)

Living contact is a vital union with God, and that means we must stay in contact with Him through prayer.

Envy is a bad enemy of love that will cause us to walk in the flesh and not in the spirit.

Envy is a feeling of discontent and ill will because of another advantage and success or possessions. Don't go there—it will take away your joy.

Sin causes us to miss the mark and keeps us from a closer walk with Christ. If you are walking in Christ, you will be able to obey the one most important commandment, and that is to love.

> *"If I speak in the tongues of men or of angels, but do not have love, I am only a resounding gong or a clanging cymbal. If I have the gift of prophecy and can fathom all mysteries and all knowledge, and if I have a faith that can move mountains, but do not have love, I am nothing. If I give all I possess to the poor and give over my body to hardship that I may boast, but do not have love, I gain nothing."*
>
> *"Love is patient, love is kind. It does not envy, it does not boast, it is not proud. It does not dishonor others, it is not self-seeking, it is not easily angered, it keeps no record of wrongs. Love does not delight in evil but rejoices with the truth. It always protects, always trusts, always hopes, always perseveres."*
>
> *"Love never fails. But where there are prophecies, they will cease; where there are tongues, they will be stilled; where there is knowledge, it will pass away."*
>
> (1 Corinthians 13:1–8 NIV)

Envy is a spirit of the devil and seems to cause us physical sickness when we don't get our way or when we don't get certain things our friends or neighbors have.

"Love does no harm to a neighbor. Therefore love is the fulfillment of the law."
(Roman 13:10 NIV)

Love causes us to fulfill all the law and the Ten Commandments.

"Therefore, rid yourselves of all malice and all deceit, hypocrisy, envy, and slander of every kind. Like newborn babies, crave pure spiritual milk, so that by it you may grow up in your salvation, now that you have tasted that the Lord is good."
(1 Peter 2:1–4 NIV)

To walk in love is to walk in the light. Put on the Lord Jesus Christ. Lay aside all guile and envious, evil speaking. Get in the Word.

"Who is wise and understanding among you? Let them show it by their good life, by deeds done in the humility that comes from wisdom. But if you harbor bitter envy and selfish ambition in your hearts, do not boast about it or deny the truth. Such "wisdom" does not come down from heaven but is earthly, unspiritual, and demonic. For where you have envy and selfish ambition, there you find disorder and every evil practice."
(James 3:13–16 NIV)

Strife is the result of envy. Strife and envy come from the devil. Where there is envy and strife there is confusion and every evil work. If there is envy and strife, you are carnal.

"Brothers and sisters, I could not address you as people who live by the Spirit but as people who are still worldly—mere infants in Christ. I gave you milk, not solid food, for you were not yet ready for it. Indeed, you are still not ready. Are you not acting like mere humans?"
(1 Corinthians 3:1–3 NIV)

"I urge you, brothers and sisters, to watch out for those who cause divisions and put obstacles in your way that are contrary to the teaching you have learned. Keep away from them."

(Romans 16:17 NIV)

Avoid those that cause divisions in your life. Yes there are those toxic people that seem to come into your life that cause your flesh come out in force, but don't let them cause you to miss your mark in the fellowship that you are striving for in walking in the Spirit.

Chase after spiritual growth in your life and a deeper walk with God and you will find what you're looking for.

Chapter 27

Juanita's Daily Prayers

"He saw that there was no one;
he was appalled that there was no one to intervene;
so his own arm achieved salvation for him,
and his own righteousness sustained him."

(Isaiah 59:16 KJV)

So God sent his Son Jesus as a mediator—He redeemed us through His blood.

We are His intercessors because of the great Intercessor.

Juanita would openly tell you and everyone around her that she was praying for them. I think we all should keep a prayer book to keep up with those that we pray for.

She felt that God was talking to her through her prayer life, and she would write them down daily to keep up with her answered prayers—and there were many.

I want to share her precious prayers of hope and faith with those that want to believe as she did. She was a prayer warrior for all those that knew her and others that will understand like I have that she just wanted the world to live in peace, have good health, and be fruitful until they are called home to be with Christ. I hope you enjoy these very private prayers from a woman who wanted a daily walk with her personal Savior.

This was taken from her Christian note-takers journal:

Goals for 1994:

- Be diligent to study and read God's Word daily
- Meditate on God's Word daily
- Pray in the Spirit more
- Intercede for our church ministry, KVTN and KVNT
- Pray for the academy
- Pray for our government leaders
- Pray for Israel
- Pray for my city and neighborhood
- Pray for the lost
- Pray for the sick
- Pray for our missionaries and other ministry
- Be diligent in my walk with God

Juanita's Daily Prayers

- Work toward excellence

- Be submissive to my husband and be a Proverbs 31 wife, the helpmate that God wanted me to be *[She didn't want to be a doormat but just a wife that stood by her husband and supported him and walked beside him and not behind him.]*

- Be diligent in my work at the store *[family-owned pharmacy]*

- Walk in Agape love *[and she did this daily]*

- Let God's Word overflow out of me to others

- I will not judge lest I be judged

- I will forgive and I will not be offended or upset at anything, even when they try to upset me

- I will walk in good health in 1994

- For I'm healed by the name of Jesus

- I will be a friend to the needy

- Will be patient and kind

May 25, 1994

These were the prayers she noted on this date. She was at her church in Little Rock, praying for her friends and family.

- Judy and Edgar: You can endure and resist the enemy *[two of her very close friends that she loved]*.

- Charlee: Endurance, encouragement—root cause—speak to it, resist the pain, Charlee. *[My daughter Charlee was in the fight of her life fighting cancer.]*

- She prayed that God would turn the President's heart in the way that he should go.

- She prayed for Janet Reno and for God to bring her to the right decision on the health care program. *I think we all need to keep praying for our government.*

- *She noted Charlee's name and this Scripture:*

  "Let us hold fast the confession of our hope without wavering; for he who promised is faithful."

  (Hebrews 10:23 KJV)

  "Therefore don't throw away your boldness, which has a great reward. For you need endurance so that, having done the will of God, you may receive the promise."

  (Hebrews 10:35–36 WEB)

  Then she wrote, "Charlee will not cast away her confidence, which hath great recompense of reward."

- Children's ministry

- Rebecca

- Provoke, to arouse, to love one another and to stimulate spiritual growth

"And I thank him who enabled me, Christ Jesus our Lord, because he counted me faithful, appointing me to service."
(1Timothy 1:12 NIV)

"Therefore lift up the hands that hang down and the feeble knees, and make straight paths for your feet, so that which is lame may not be dislocated, but rather be healed. Follow after peace with all men, and the sanctification without which no man will see the Lord."
(Hebrews 12:14 WEB)

- Russell and Patti to be strong in their faith during these hard times

- Juanita, you will follow peace unto all men.

July 21, 1994

- Gift of faith for Charlee *[She was blessed with the gift of faith and she never gave up on her belief through many dark days of her illness].*

- Dudley strength *[Dudley was fighting heart disease at the time of this prayer. She wrote this Scripture down by her husband's name.].*

"He gives strength to the weary and increases the power of the weak. Even youths grow tired and weary, and young men stumble and fall; but those who hope in the LORD will renew their strength."

"They will soar on wings like eagles; they will run and not grow weary; they will walk and not be faint."

(Isaiah 40:29–31 NIV)

- Patti's strength *[Patti was Juanita's—daughter and my wife]*

"If anyone speaks, let it be as it were the very words of God. If anyone serves, let it be as of the strength which God supplies, that in all things God may be glorified through Jesus Christ, to whom belong the glory and the dominion forever and ever. Amen."

(1 Peter 4:11 NIV)

- Russell *[Most of the time she was praying for me to have wisdom, and to be successful in my career. Well, I'm still working on both. Oh, and by the way, I have a great job, and Juanita prayed me into some of the best jobs in the world. When you have a mother-in-law like Nita, you are going to be blessed. God has blessed me in so many ways. With a few more years, maybe the wisdom will come along. I know my wife can't wait for this one to come along.]*

"I keep asking that the God of our Lord Jesus Christ, the glorious Father, may give you the Spirit of wisdom and revelation, so that you may know him better. I pray that the eyes of your heart may be enlightened in order that you may know the hope to which he has called you, the riches of his glorious inheritance in his holy people, and his incomparably great power for us who believe. That power is the same as the mighty strength."

(Ephesians 1:17–19 JKV)

- Judy and Edgar. I pray for them on their trip to Ireland. *[Juanita loved younger couples and loved to mentor and care for them]*.

- My God supplies all mine and Dudley's needs.

September 3, 1994

Mercy—compassion to those that are condemned or suffering—forgiveness

"Therefore I tell you, whatever you ask for in prayer, believe that you have received it, and it will be yours."

(Mark 11:24 NIV)

January 3, 1994

- Denton to have Godly friends [*My son and Juanita's Grandson*].

When I was a young man I was about as wild as you could get. I had those friends who wanted to run wild and those who just wanted to trust God. I've been extremely blessed to have a longtime friend from back in the seventies that came to my rescue when I got myself in a big mess. He stood by me by taking time to be a friend and a mentor, until I found my way.

What a great friend he was to take time to share with someone who really was in need. We all need Godly friends like my longtime friend, Rick Greer. He came to share his faith with me and helped me through a very dark time in my life. We all need to take time to be a Godly friend to those that find themselves in a fiery situation and need help to extinguish problems that can consume every part of their lives.

- Charlee to have physical strength to climb stairs [*Here she is declaring the works of the Lord.*]

- Russell to pray

- We must be determined to do what God shows us to do to receive our Jubilee.

- Denton being healed of his sunburn

May 23, 1995

- Jack's healing *[Jack was Juanita's brother who she loved dearly.]*

On May 27, 1995, she noted the fruit of the Spirit and this:

- Love suffers long and is kind

- Does not envy

- Is not puffed up

- Does not behave rudely

- Does not seek its own and is not provoked, thinks no evil, does not rejoice in iniquity but rejoices in truth

- Bares all things

- Hopes all things

- Endures all things

- Never fails

August 29, 1995

- Mark to hear God's voice 8/29/95. *Juanita tried to teach all her family and friends to take time each day to listen to God's spirit, so that He could convey to us the blueprint of how we should live and interact with the world that we live in.*

September 7, 1995

- Lord, help me to endure persecutions. I believe that you are able to deliver me out of any situation.

- For Patti to have wisdom with her scheduling so she doesn't take on too much work. *The reason for her scheduling problems was a very sick child and a creative ability with fabric.*

- This is a perilous time. It is not a time to be playing around, but it is time to be totally committed, sold out to God. It is urgent to be obedient to the Word of God *[All I can think of is, "Oh, my God, she knew how to pray." Wow. If we all took a few minutes each day, how we could change the world.].*

- Lord, I commit myself totally to you—I sell out to you. Help me, Lord, not to let the things of the world touch me or latch onto me.

- I want to walk more and more with You, Lord

- Show me, Father, what I need to get rid of.

- I will praise you more each day.

- I will study and meditate on Your Word each day. I will listen to the Word each day. I will cut out secular TV each day.

January 1, 1996

- I will walk in your peace and joy each day. I will lift up Jesus to all people each day. I will talk of your wondrous works, Lord, each day. This is the year for Victory.

- God is Jehovah Jireh, our Provider.

"Dear friend, I pray that you may enjoy good health and that all may go well with you, even as your soul is getting along well. It gave me great joy when some believers came and testified about your faithfulness to the truth, telling how you continue to walk in it. I have no greater joy than to hear that my children are walking in the truth."

1 John1, 2 NIV)

"He who has pity on the poor lends to the Lord, and he will pay back what he has given."

(Proverbs 19:17 NKJV)

"But remember the Lord your God, for it is he who gives you the ability to produce wealth, and so confirms his covenant, which he swore to your ancestors, as it is today."

(Deuteronomy 8:18 NIV)

My wife and I are just amazed at how many prayers are answered each day. Just a few months ago, Betty, the mother of one of our high school classmates, Robin Berry, was in the hospital because she had become very sick.

Robin posted on social media that his mother was sick, and he needed all of his friends to say a prayer for her. Within a short time, Robin reported that each time someone responded to his social media post, a bell would ring. He immediately told his mother what was going on and noticed how excited his mother got. Each and every time she heard that bell ring, she seemed to get a little better. It wasn't long before Miss Betty was doing a whole lot better and was out of the hospital. My wife saw her the other day in the grocery store and was amazed at how well she was doing.

Oh, how much power is out there for us to tap into if we all get together, unite as one, and ask for a little help? When someone asks you to pray for him or her, really take time to step into the presence of God and ask for His help.

Chapter 28

Peace of God

"In nothing be anxious, but in everything, by prayer and petition with thanksgiving, let your requests be made known to God. And the peace of God, which surpasses all understanding, will guard your hearts and your thoughts in Christ Jesus."

"Finally, brothers, whatever things are true, whatever things are honorable, whatever things are just, whatever things are pure, whatever things are lovely, whatever things are of good report; if there is any virtue, and if there is any praise, think about these things. The things which you learned, received, heard, and saw in me: do these things and the God of peace will be with you. But I rejoice in the Lord greatly, that now at length you have revived your thought for me; in which you did indeed take thought, but you lacked opportunity."

(Philippians 4:6–10 WEB)

Make your requests known, and then trust God that He has heard your prayers and has already answered them.

"Humble yourselves therefore under the mighty hand of God, that he may exalt you in due time; casting all your worries on him, because he cares for you."

(1 Peter 5:6–7 WEB)

Whenever you felt confused or worried, Juanita would share these simple truths with you. She did with me on many occasions and coming from a back ground of confusion and strife in the home, I needed this reassurance from an seasoned Christian She would share her confidence and wisdom with everyone that came asking.

As we cast our care on the Lord, when things are upsetting us, causing us to be anxious, the minute we cast it on Him, the Lord's peace will come to set us free. Take time each day to focus on His thoughts.

> "*Do not work for food that spoils, but for food that endures to eternal life, which the Son of Man will give you. For on him God the Father has placed his seal of approval.*"
>
> (John 6:27 NIV)

Don't just work for food because food will perish and His life-sustaining food is the Spirit that will last forever. Trust in Him and all your needs will be met. Jesus is the Word made flesh and provides us with spiritual food. Peace and tranquility will come into our spiritual man once we eat of the bread of heaven, which is the Word of God.

Jesus took a few fish and a small amount of bread and fed thousands. Jesus wanted to share more than a meal to those men and women who came to hear him speak. He wanted to give them a more abundant life filled with His peace. Do you have days when you just don't have the joy and peace that you should have? Take a deep breath and ask God for a little help. It's right there waiting, for you. All you have to do is believe that you will receive it.

> "Philip answered him, "Two hundred denarii worth of bread is not sufficient for them, that every one of them may receive a little."

"One of his disciples, Andrew, Simon Peter's brother, said to him, "There is a boy here who has five barley loaves and two fish, but what are these among so many?"

"Jesus said, "Have the people sit down." Now there was much grass in that place. So the men sat down, in number about five thousand. Jesus took the loaves; and having given thanks, he distributed to the disciples, and the disciples to those who were sitting down; likewise also of the fish as much as they desired. When they were filled, he said to his disciples, "Gather up the broken pieces which are left over, that nothing is lost. "So they gathered them up, and filled twelve baskets with broken pieces from the five barley loaves, which were left over by those who had eaten."

(John 6:7–13 NIV)

"Therefore, beloved, seeing that you look for these things, be diligent to be found in peace, without defect and blameless in his sight."

(2 Peter 3:14 WEB)

Can our Father find peace in us?

"You will keep whoever's mind is steadfast in perfect peace, because he trusts in you."

(Isaiah 26:3 WEB)

God will keep us in this perfect peace when we keep our minds staying on him. As we keep our mind stayed on our Lord, we have the peace and tranquility that we need as we walk in this world.

"Don't be conformed to this world, but be transformed by the renewing of your mind, so that you may prove what is the good, well-pleasing, and perfect will of God."

(Romans 12:2 WEB)

We just need to tell our mouths to confess His word.

> *"But the Counselor, the Holy Spirit, whom the Father will send in my name, he will teach you all things, and will remind you of all that I said to you. Peace I leave with you. My peace I give to you; not as the world gives, give I to you. Don't let your heart be troubled, neither let it be fearful."*
>
> (John 14:26, 27 WEB)

> *"I have told you these things, so that in me you may have peace. In this world you will have trouble. But take heart! I have overcome the world."*
>
> (John 16:33 NIV)

In Him you will have peace. My peace slipped away when I was building my second house. I had finished nailing the last board at the very top of the gable end of the house when the ladder I was on decided to slide off the roof. It was a very long fall from that roof. I landed on both feet, and one of my ankles was broken as I hit the ground. It was a trip to the hospital. After the broken ankle was set, a little worry set in. My wife bought me a red shirt and added a picture of a man with just a few hairs on his head and the words to my favorite song... "Don't worry, be happy."

Don't-worry-be-happy was not what I was thinking at that point. I thought instead, "How will I finish this house?" After a few weeks, it was time to stop the worry. I went out on a faith-limb and started controlling the thoughts that were coming into my head. The song "Don't Worry, Be Happy" kept coming into my head: I had to get going. I sat on a five-gallon container and starting laying hardwood flooring. My second house did get completed after a few months. We moved in on concrete floors and finished it after a few months. Guess what? You can do all things in Christ who gives you the strength.

"He came and preached peace to you who were far off and to those who were near."

(Ephesians 2:17 WEB)

Jesus is our peace.

Jesus made peace by the blood of the cross and by giving Himself for the world as a perfect sacrifice.

"For all the fullness was pleased to dwell in him; and through him to reconcile all things to himself, by him, whether things on the earth, or things in the heavens, having made peace through the blood of his cross."

"You, being in past times alienated and enemies in your mind in your evil deeds, yet now he has reconciled in the body of his flesh through death, to present you holy and without defect and blameless before him, if it is so that you continue in the faith, grounded and steadfast, and not moved away from the hope of the Good News which you heard, which is being proclaimed in all creation under heaven; of which I, Paul, was made a servant."

"Now I rejoice in my sufferings for your sake, and fill up on my part that which is lacking of the afflictions of Christ in my flesh for his body's sake, which is the assembly; of which I was made a servant, according to the stewardship of God which was given me toward you, to fulfill the word of God, the mystery which has been hidden for ages and generations. But now it has been revealed to his saints, to whom God was pleased to make known what are the riches of the glory of this mystery among the Gentiles, which is Christ in you, the hope of glory; whom we proclaim, admonishing every man and teaching every man in all wisdom, that we may present every man perfect in Christ Jesus;

for which I also labor, striving according to his working, which works in me mightily."

(Colossians 1:19–29 WEB)

Do you wonder if God is trying to reveal Himself to you? Keep seeking His wisdom and love and you will find yourself more perfect in Christ.

Chapter 29

Tasso

"Story" by Coby Smith

*"Take delight in the Lord,
and he will give you the desires of your heart."*

—Psalm 37:4 (NIV)

It was September 2005. I was in a rut and had been for years. I drank too much. I was looking for love in all the wrong places. My biggest problem was that I was lonely. I wanted what most people wanted. I wanted to fall in love and find my wife. I had been in many relationships, but there was no one I could call my wife so far.

I lived with a woman for several years. She had two kids. I knew I was never going to marry her. I really felt sorry for her children, so I stayed around a lot longer than I should have. My mother couldn't stand this woman. My mom has always wanted the best for me. She knew that there was someone out there who was better for me. I was finally ready to make a break from this woman, so I called my mom and told her that I wanted to move back home. Not many mothers would want their twenty-eight-year-old son moving back home, but my mom would do anything for me to get out of that relationship.

So at twenty-eight, I moved home with my mother. It was quite depressing, but I was finally free. I still went to bars and did the things that I shouldn't be doing. Many days and nights, I would sit and pray. I would beg God to help me find a wife. My mother was also praying that I would find someone who loved me.

One of the conditions of me living at my mother's house was that I had to pay rent. I had to pay her five hundred dollars per paycheck. That was about half of what I was bringing home. I was chef at the time, and I worked for a catering company. I worked strange hours at all different locations.

Every year, we would complete a catering order for a local chapter of Ducks Unlimited. This particular year, I was lucky enough to attend the event. I went early to set everything up, and then I had enough time to go home, take a shower, and attend the event as a guest. These DU banquets are set up to make money. They serve a lot of beer and then entice you to bid on different items. After almost everyone is a bit tipsy, Ducks Unlimited begins a live auction. Some of the items that year were a couple of Labrador retrievers, or duck dogs. There was a female golden retriever and a male black Labrador retriever. I had always wanted a duck dog. The female was up first. The bidding started, and I threw my hand up. There were several bidders, and the price was going up. In my inebriated state, I had set my limit at three hundred dollars. As the bidding went up, it finally reached the three-hundred-dollar mark. The auctioneer looked directly at me and asked if I would make another bid. I looked around and decided that I had had enough. I said no. To my surprise, the auctioneer looked at me again and said, "Would you bid three hundred for the other dog?" Again I looked around. Everyone was staring at me. I was just drunk enough that I said, "Hell yeah!" So I won the dog. Here I was, living with my parents, and I had just won a dog. I was thinking to myself, "How in the world am I going to pull this off?"

When I got home that night, I knew what my mother's reaction was going to be. She was not going to be happy. The story that I came up with was that I had just won the dog. I never told her how I won the dog. She didn't need to know that it happened during an auction. She was still not very happy with me. She immediately told me to get rid of the dog, but by this time, the dog had a name: Tasso. Tasso is a Cajun-cured ham. Since I was a chef, I thought the name was perfect. My mother was still not impressed. After I had Tasso for a week or so, my mother told me that I had to move out. At this point, I was in love with my dog. I wasn't getting rid of Tasso, and I also ignored my mother's request about moving out.

Every day after work, I would come home, get Tasso, and go for a ride. Tasso loved the car. We would go to the lake and play fetch. He loved to go swimming. We would also go to the dog park. We were pretty much inseparable. I finally had something more important than myself, and my mother started taking notice. She began realizing that this dog was slowly changing me and that Tasso was making me somewhat more responsible. Instead of going to happy hour after work, I started going to different dog parks in the area. It didn't take me very long to figure out that lots of single women also went to dog parks.

On a September afternoon, I took notice of a young lady. She had a dog named Chox. Our dogs hit it off pretty well. We chatted for a few minutes. It was getting dark, and the bugs were coming out. She went her way, and I went mine. After we left, I was kicking myself, asking myself why didn't I ask her out. To my surprise, the girl was right in front of me as we were driving. I told myself that if given the chance, I would ask her out.

Just as I thought this, she put her blinker on to turn into the gas station. My heart thumped. I followed and pulled up beside her. I told her that I should have asked her out at the dog park and that I didn't want to miss another opportunity. She gave me her number. I immediately thought she could be the one. She just seemed so sweet and caring.

After a few days, I called her. We chatted for a while, and then I set up a date. Our first date was September 16, 2006. We had a really good time. We continued to date. Our dogs became best friends, just as we were becoming best friends.

My mother knew that this girl could be the one. Sometime in August that next year, she asked me what I planned to do. I told her that I needed to save some money to buy a ring. That's when my mother dropped the bomb: she told me that all the money I had been paying in rent was waiting for me in a savings account. She told me that I had nearly twenty thousand dollars. I was shocked. I was able to begin looking for rings immediately.

Exactly one year to the day, on September 16, 2007, I proposed to the girl of my dreams. We were married on May 2, 2008.

There are many things in this world that I don't know, but I do know that God sent me an angel in the form of a dog named Tasso. Tasso helped me grow up. He helped me understand what I am capable of in life. Tasso probably saved my life. Thank God for my dog.

Tasso

A few days after Coby gave me this story about Tasso, he said, "Russell, let me tell you what we did with Tasso's ashes." *He went on to say,* "My family and I drove to our favorite lake and went out in our boat to the small island we call Hamburger Island, since the shape of it looked a lot like a hamburger. I decided to leave his ashes at our favorite lake, where we had so many memorable adventures. I would throw a tennis ball out wherever we were, and he would fetch it back to me; the game of fetch would go on for hours.

"The lake was smooth as glass that day, and the lake was calm as I had ever seen it. As I threw out his ashes in the lake, all I could do is remember how much he helped me through some very tough times and just how much joy he brought back into my life.

"To remember one more good time, I threw out a tennis ball and then his ashes. After his ashes settled on top of the lake, they seemed to take on the shape of a dog balled up asleep. Wow! I know that is wild, but that is what I saw, and it was his image. Then all of a sudden, a few hundred small fish came up to our boat and just looked at me. I know at that point, Tasso was saying good-bye. God has been so good to me, and all I want to do is thank Him for the angel of a dog named Tasso. He came into my life and saved me from being just a wandering young man without a family of my own. That old wonderful dog caused me to think about someone else greater than just myself. Because of that lab, I have two great kids and a wife who actually loves me.

"I know God was speaking to me and my family as we shared that moment in time. Prayers are answered in so many ways. I know God sent me a gift that changed my life for the better, and it was Tasso."

Chapter 30

Jesus Gives Us Peace

"Peace I leave with you. My peace I give to you; not as the world gives, give I to you. Don't let your heart be troubled, neither let it be fearful."
(John 14:27 WEB)

Jesus said, "I leave peace with you." Jesus always left peace, and people felt calm and at peace.

Do people feel the peace of Jesus in us as we are around them, or do we leave them confused and upset with what we left them?

Jesus walked the perfect walk here on earth—so can we do the same? Jesus died that we might have life and have it more abundantly. "More abundantly" comes as we allow Him to show us how we are to walk.

To be perfect in the love of Christ is our motivation.

Christians walk in the perfect faith-walk with Him. It's all about one thing—believing that He is—and your faith will carry you the rest of the way.

> "See to it that no one takes you captive through hollow and deceptive philosophy, which depends on human tradition and the elemental spiritual forces of this world rather than on Christ."
>
> "For in Christ all the fullness of the Deity lives in bodily form."
>
> (Colossians 2:8, 9 NIV)

Surrender everything you have so you can have that completed walk in Him and the peace that will take you all the way to the finish line.

> "In whom you were also circumcised with a circumcision not made with hands, in the putting off of the body of the sins of the flesh, in the circumcision of Christ."
>
> (Colossians 2:11 NIV)

> "In whom we have our redemption, the forgiveness of our sins."
>
> (Colossians 1:14 NIV)

> "For God was pleased to have all his fullness dwell in him, and through him to reconcile to himself all things, whether things on earth or things in heaven, by making peace through his blood, shed on the cross. Once you were alienated from God and were enemies in your minds because of your evil behavior. But now he has reconciled you by Christ's physical body through death to present you holy in his sight, without blemish and free from accusation—if you continue in your faith, established and firm, and do not move from the hope held out in the gospel. This is the gospel that you heard and that has been proclaimed to every creature under heaven, and of which I, Paul, have become a servant."
>
> (Colossians 1:19–23 NIV)

We can experience His peace once we change directions, and we ask for a little help. If you have guilt in your life, there is no peace. Make a change in your life, and go the other direction to remove the guilt that is slowing you down.

> "In whom are all the treasures of wisdom and knowledge hidden."
> (Colossians 2:3 WEB)

> "Be wise in the way you act toward outsiders; make the most of every opportunity. Let your conversation be always full of grace, seasoned with salt, so that you may know how to answer everyone."
> (Colossians 4:5–6 NIV)

> "For though I am absent in the flesh, yet am I with you in the spirit, rejoicing and seeing your order, and the steadfastness of your faith in Christ."
> (Colossians 2:5)

> "My goal is that they may be encouraged in heart and united in love, so that they may have the full riches of complete understanding, in order that they may know the mystery of God, namely, Christ, in whom are hidden all the treasures of wisdom and knowledge. I tell you this so that no one may deceive you by fine-sounding arguments."
> (Colossians 2:4 NIV)

Faith in Christ is the objective to strive for.

> "As therefore you received Christ Jesus, the Lord, walk in him, rooted and built up in him, and established in the faith, even as you were taught, abounding in it in thanksgiving."
> (Colossians 2:6–7 WEB)

"Grandma's story "By Sara and David Rhoads

My Mom (Martha Jean Rhoads) was diagnosed with cancer on October 1, 2013. Starting on October 2, she started witnessing to everyone at the hospital who came into her room or she passed by in the hallway. She required that every doctor had prayer with her. She started her journey with cancer with a positive attitude. The doctors gave her six months to live. The Lord gave her nine months to share with the world. One month after leaving the hospital, she was cooking for her neighbors who were ill. She made the very best of it. She never gave up. She ended her journey with a positive attitude. That attitude was "I am going to be with the Lord." The words that follow were written by my daughter Sarah the day after my Mom died on June 13. This was her eulogy for her Grandma Rhoads.

The definition of strength for me is three words: Martha Jean Rhoads. Grandma was a woman who was hardheaded, loved to work in her yard, and go for walks even if it was at 2:00 a.m. She had an unwavering faith in God and never doubted for one second what happened after this life.

She was a rock for me when I needed someone to tell my secrets to, always there to make sure I was on the right path and the best therapist/listener love could buy. She never let anyone she loved have cold feet or leave extra catfish on their plate. There was no need to be wasteful in her mind.

The caring heart, never ending love, and ability to make people laugh are the things that made her one of my favorites. Grandma most days had more energy and determination than I do. It's something I always admired about her. She never complained about anything even when the road got bumpy. She always had a smile on her face and a hug waiting on you. There are too many reasons to list why I love her and am forever grateful to her.

The thing I will always be forever grateful for is the fact that she gave me a daddy who's the perfect combination of her and Grandpa. I see so much of her in not only my dad but in my uncles also. I don't think they could have done a better job raising their boys and I know even now she's looking down and thinking we did something right. I like to think I'm a pretty lucky girl in the uncle/dad department. They have taken everything Grandma and Grandpa taught them and instilled in us the same morals and I hope to do the same with my kids one day. Saying goodbye is never something anyone enjoys so I refuse to say goodbye to you, just see you later. Grandma, I will love and miss you forever.

I know Grandpa has an unlimited supply of catfish waiting on you and that everyone else will be walking around in knitted booties in no time. I will always love you pretty lady.

Chapter 31

Randy

"By Wanda Hitt, Randy's mother"

Ever since I can remember, drugs and alcohol were ever present, as if the family was dead and the buzzards circled around and over us with the two evils.

I was an average girl growing up, without parents, and always getting myself into trouble, which resulted in my having to be moved to another relative. My grandparents took care of me as long as they were able. I moved to Northern California and then on to Southern California. (Those are different stories to be told some day.) I married on March 11, 1962, had twin boys February 18, 1963, followed by my daughter on February 18, 1965. My baby son, Randy Michael Wooten, was born August 29, 1966.

Somewhere between the ages of twelve and fourteen, Randy began drinking. Nineteen eighty was the year of my divorce from his father, and for many years before the divorce my husband or I did not set a very good example for him—except in the drugs and the drinking. We openly had parties that had alcohol as well as drugs present for the entire world to see, and unfortunately my children saw it all up close.

When I left, Randy stayed with his father—who married again thirty days later. The parties continued, so the example did not stop. Randy told me once that he used to go to his cousins' house, and they allowed him to have beer. He would stagger home to his aunt and uncle's home, get in bed, and be so drunk that he couldn't even get up to go to the bathroom.

Randy had various jobs—construction jobs, janitor-type positions—and he helped me with jobs I might have. But he was an alcoholic with his drugs of choice.

Randy married a young lady who had two children, the youngest a girl. They partied with her children present. Randy was physically mean to this woman. Of course, that ended in divorce.

He married twice more and both women brought children into the marriages.

Randy made his way in and out of jails and prisons most of his life. In 2005, Randy was sentenced to seven years in prison for his connection to drugs. He spent four and a half years of his life in a state institution and was then transferred to a federal correctional facility for possession of a firearm connected to the state drug charge.

He transferred himself to the federal El Reno Correctional Facility in Oklahoma where Jesus led him to a good group of people. He began to attend church every time the doors were opened, and he was allowed to attend. He gave his life to Jesus there in that prison and was baptized.

Randy

> *"Therefore, if anyone is in Christ, he is a new creation. The old has passed away; behold, the new has come. All this is from God, who through Christ reconciled us to himself and gave us the ministry of reconciliation; that is, in Christ God was reconciling the world to himself, not counting their trespasses against them, and entrusting to us the message of reconciliation. Therefore, we are ambassadors for Christ, God making his appeal through us. We implore you on behalf of Christ, be reconciled to God. For our sake he made him to be sin who knew no sin, so that in him we might become the righteousness of God."*
>
> (1 Corinthians 5:17–21 ESV)

About the same time I remarried and was led to Christ myself. Our faith grew together. Our letters were full of the future and how he planned to get out, attend church, and live his life for Jesus. His goal was to spread God's Word and use his experience of the past to demonstrate to others that all things were possible through our Lord Jesus Christ. His desire was to bring his brothers and sister to know the Lord. He had some interaction with his sister, and they had planned on moving to the Arkansas area.

I was so overjoyed by Randy's new found Friend, Jesus Christ. He did not send a letter to me without mentioning what happened in the services at the prison. I had been praying for Randy for all his years of life. I prayed things would change and that he would find peace, joy, and comfort. I was raised in a Church of God (Pentecostal), so I knew the Lord. I had asked for forgiveness of my sins and began to attend church with friends. I was working at a job in Texas, driving back and forth to Arkansas on the weekends. I would stop by Randy's job on my way home and visit with him. I could see him going downhill through things that were going on at his job. God has blessed me all of my life. I cannot express enough that, because of my raising, I knew God was there even though I ignored that fact most of the time. I began to renew my relationship with the Lord Jesus Christ, and I continued to pray for my son.

So you can imagine how grieved I was by the news I received on November 30, 2011: Randy was diagnosed with lung cancer, stage three. Randy was due to be released March 7. With this news I began to try to get him out of there. I was told he would do every minute of his time. Randy began to get progressively worse, but he said, "Mama, be sure to tell my friend who is already out not to blame God. God didn't do this to me—I did." He worried about his young friend, Nick, but he had the opportunity to tell him on the phone those very words.

Randy's chemotherapy began in that same prison, the federal El Reno Correctional Facility. He began to experience low blood counts, so they had to stop the therapy. Cancer was growing rapidly. The next thing I knew, he was being transferred to the federal "hospital prison," Butner in North Carolina. His bone marrow would not produce red and white blood cells. I talked with several doctors and case workers. They were so helpful and supportive to me during this time. The case worker made arrangements to have Randy flown to directly to UAMS in Little Rock on March 7, 2012, his release date. Randy and I stayed at the hospital from that date until March 22, 2012, when he went home with hospice.

Randy went home to be with Jesus April 2, 2012. I'm telling this story because our heavenly Father loves each one of us. No matter where we come from or what we do, he will forgive us. Randy made a great impression on his friends at the prison. They all called, wrote, and had their families call me to find out how Randy was making it when he was transferred. Even if they were prisoners, they loved our Lord Jesus Christ and were brothers in Christ with Randy.

Randy

With tears in my eyes I cannot tell you how angels walk in those prisons. They are a lost people to 75 percent of this world. They have no one but God, and I am so glad God was with my son.

Chapter 32

How to Be Perfect in Your Love Walk

God's love was put inside us when we were born again as new creations. The Word says we are created in the image of God. When the Holy Spirit came to dwell in our spirit, we had a baptism of love—God is love, and because the Holy Spirit is the third person of the Trinity, He is Love. Now the Holy Spirit may dwell in us, but we may not be letting Him have full reign over our lives to let God love through us.

> *"A new command I give you: Love one another. As I have loved you, so you must love one another. By this everyone will know that you are my disciples, if you love one another."*
>
> (John 13:34, 35 NIV)

Now let us each examine and judge ourselves on this: unless we judge ourselves, we will be judged. Do we really love one another? This is all God's children. Now it's pretty easy to love those we don't come in contact with. But what about those we are so closely associated with, say other people in our prayer group? We're not perfected yet, so when one of us says something the other doesn't like, etc., we might think,

"I just can't love that person." Wrong. That is not the right confession to make.

We *can* love them—though Christ who gives us the strength to do something our fleshly man does not want to do.

Cast down those hateful critical thoughts and those words that slip out. And how they slip out! I have to ask forgiveness just about every few minutes during the day. If you remember I'm the sinner who wrote this book and most likely will have to keep working on this one to improve my walk with God.

Even though I'm a sinner, I have a get out of hell card called the redeemed card, through Christ giving Himself for the world as the one and only begotten Son. He was the perfect sacrifice for me and everyone that wants to change and become Christ like.

> "But I tell you, love your enemies and pray for those who persecute you."
> (Matthew 5:44 NIV)

Be the one that breaks the curse that follows all of us and our families by blessing those who hate you.

Saying bad things about each other does not cause you to love one another. And saying bad things about others can come very easy for a lot of people.

> "Seeing you have purified your souls in your obedience to the truth through the Spirit in sincere brotherly affection, love one another from the heart fervently."
> (1 Peter 1:22 KJV)

> "You, dear children, are from God and have overcome them, because the one who is in you is greater than the one who is in the world.

They are from the world and therefore speak from the viewpoint of the world, and the world listens to them. We are from God, and whoever knows God listens to us; but whoever is not from God does not listen to us. This is how we recognize the Spirit of truth and the spirit of falsehood."

"Dear friends, let us love one another, for love comes from God. Everyone who loves has been born of God and knows God. Whoever does not love does not know God, because God is love. This is how God showed his love among us: He sent his one and only Son into the world that we might live through him. This is love: not that we loved God, but that he loved us and sent his Son as an atoning sacrifice for our sins. Dear friends, since God so loved us, we also ought to love one another. No one has ever seen God; but if we love one another, God lives in us and his love is made complete in us."

"This is how we know that we live in him and He in us: He has given us of his Spirit. And we have seen and testify that the Father has sent His Son to be the Savior of the world. If anyone acknowledges that Jesus is the Son of God, God lives in them and they in God. And so we know and rely on the love God has for us."

"God is love. Whoever lives in love lives in God, and God in them. This is how love is made complete among us so that we will have confidence on the Day of Judgment: In this world we are like Jesus. There is no fear in love. But perfect love drives out fear, because fear has to do with punishment. The one who fears is not made perfect in love."

"We love because He first loved us. Whoever claims to love God yet hates a brother or sister is a liar. For whoever does not love their brother and sister, whom they have seen, cannot love God, whom they have not seen. And he has given us this command: Anyone who loves God must also love their brother and sister."

(1 John 4:4–21 NIV)

1. Love one another, and treat each other as brothers and sister in Christ.

2. Love your enemies—pray for them that speak evil.

3. Don't listen to Satan's lies about the saints. He is forever accusing each of us to each other and to God—don't listen to the lies.

4. The more time we spend in God's Word, the more this will crowd out the impurities that seem to drift into our lives. Be washed by the Word, and then love can flow freely.

5. Praying in the Spirit edifies. Build up this power and love that is with us.

6. When God tells you to do something, do it with love—don't grumble and gripe.

7. Walk in the love God has shed abroad in our hearts. As we walk He matures us. Halleluiah!

> *"But the fruit of the Spirit is love, joy, peace, forbearance, kindness, goodness, faithfulness."*
>
> (Galatians 5:22 NIV)

The fruit is a bud first. Then it becomes a blossom, and then a tiny fruit. Finally it matures into ripe fruit.

Some of us are still in the bud stage of the fruit of love. We need to let it burst forth and make fruit—to ripen and mature.

We shouldn't listen to Satan's lies about each other so that it won't slow our growth in Christ.

> *"For this reason I kneel before the Father, from whom every family in heaven and on earth derives its name. I pray that out of his glorious riches he may strengthen you with power through his Spirit in your inner being, so that Christ may dwell in your hearts through faith. And I pray that you, being rooted and established in love, may have power, together with all the Lord's holy people, to grasp how wide and long and high and deep is the love of Christ, and to know this love that surpasses knowledge—that you may be filled to the measure of all the fullness of God."*
> (Ephesians 3:14–19 NIV)

The Love of Christ passes even our own knowledge.

Paul in these verses is conveying that He wants us to know the height, depth, breadth, and length of God's love.

The love of Christ surpasses all that has been known ("knowledge"). This means a body wholly filled—totally and completely. Paul was writing to Spirit-filled Christians. We need to be so full of God's love that it shows without saying a word.

> *"Remembering without ceasing your work of faith and labor of love and patience of hope in our Lord Jesus Christ, before our God and Father."*
> (1 Thessalonians 1:3)

There should be such a bond of love between us that it motivates us to help each other.

God gives us the spirit of power, of love, and of self-control.

God has given this to us, but the minute we entertain any unloving thought—and then let it fall out of our mouths—Satan has a toehold. And that causes an opening for him to enter into our lives.

Chapter 33

Perfecting Our Love Walk

"Therefore if anyone is in Christ, he is a new creation. The old things have passed away. Behold all things have become new."

(2 Corinthians 5:17 NIV)

Becoming a new creature in Christ should be our main goal in life. We are new creatures. We have the Spirit of God dwelling in us. We have an advocate, the Lord Jesus Christ, when we sin. He is faithful and just to forgive us. The world can't come against us when we have God's Spirit in us.

"Be therefore imitators of God, as beloved children. Walk in love, even as Christ also loved you, and gave himself up for us, an offering and a sacrifice to God for a sweet-smelling fragrance."

(Ephesians 5: 1–2 WEB)

Walk in love as Christ also hath loved us.

"No one has seen God at any time. If we love one another, God remains in us, and his love has been perfected in us."

"By this we know that we remain in him and He in us, because He has given us of his Spirit. We have seen and testify that the Father has sent the Son as the Savior of the world. Whoever confesses that Jesus is the Son of God, God remains in Him, and He in God. We know and have believed the love which God has for us. God is love, and he who remains in love remains in God, and God remains in him. In this love has been made perfect among us, that we may have boldness in the day of judgment, because as he is, even so are we in this world. There is no fear in love; but perfect love casts out fear, because fear has punishment. He who fears is not made perfect in love. We love him, because he first loved us. If a man says, "I love God," and hates his brother, he is a liar; for he who doesn't love his brother whom he has seen, how can he love God whom he has not seen? This commandment we have from him, that he who loves God should also love his brother."

(1 John 4:12–21 WEB)

We are to walk, act, and confess love, which is the Word of God.

"My children, I will be with you only a little longer. You will look for me, and just as I told the Jews, so I tell you now: Where I am going, you cannot come.

"A new command I give you: Love one another. As I have loved you, so you must love one another. By this everyone will know that you are my disciples, if you love one another."

(John 13:33–35 NIV)

This can be very hard to do when you're around people who just drive you crazy. I have to take a deep breath, and ask for a little help from God each day and most of us do. I know if I place all my thoughts on Christ I'll have a good day. Putting Juanita's notes into this book has really helped me look at myself daily. We can really mess things up with our relationships with people when we do not truly love and care for people like Christ wants us too. Love the ones that drive you crazy and you might want to stay a distance from them to keep your sanity.

Perfecting Our Love Walk

1. Jesus said it—we are to love one another.

2. We are to operate and walk in love. *I have to work on this every day.*

2. We cannot hurt others if we use words that are filled with God's love.

We do not talk critical about others, we do not judge another—why would I do such a thing? We have no fear in Christ once we believe in Him. The love of God is in us. We know He is our Father. He is our caretaker. Once we accept Jesus, we are no longer afraid of what people can do to us.

> *"Are not all angels ministering spirits sent to serve those who will inherit salvation?"*
>
> (Hebrew 1:14 NIV)

Angel protection is there for us. All we have to do is ask for their help.

We don't have to fear about money.

We are outside the realm of sin.

When the love of God is in us, walking and operating through us, we do not sin.

Walk above evil in the world.

God is in us, and we have His Word: "I will fear no evil."

Confess love

"If I speak in the tongues of men or of angels, but do not have love, I am only a resounding gong or a clanging cymbal. If I have the gift of prophecy and can fathom all mysteries and all knowledge, and if I have a faith that can move mountains, but do not have love, I am nothing. If I give all I possess to the poor and give over my body to hardship that I may boast but do not have love, I gain nothing."

"Love is patient, love is kind. It does not envy, it does not boast, it is not proud. It does not dishonor others, it is not self-seeking, it is not easily angered, and it keeps no record of wrongs. Love does not delight in evil but rejoices with the truth. It always protects, always trusts, always hopes, and always perseveres."

"Love never fails. But where there are prophecies, they will cease; where there are tongues, they will be stilled; where there is knowledge, it will pass away."

(1 Corinthians 13:1–8 NIV)

If we have not love, the gifts won't do any good. God gives His followers gifts.

Where there is love-consciousness, there is no self-consciousness.

We are not worried about what people think of us. But we have cut the umbilical cord that once joined us to the world. We will always boldly pray for those that are not connected to God so they can become children of God.

Love forgives

"And when you stand praying, if you hold anything against anyone, forgive them, so that your Father in heaven may forgive you your sins."

(Mark 11:25 NIV)

When we take a stand and pray for others this opens up the channel to God, which keeps the love operating in us.

Love keeps its mouth shut. Jesus at the trial opens not His mouth. The good news is He came to give His life for us, and that's why there was not a word spoken. He was the perfect sacrifice for all mankind.

Don't be a carrier of bad news and bad reports. *We all can be guilty of this—and maybe that's another reason for the subtitle of this book—I'm far from a saint. As I put this book together, I feel the Holy Spirit is bringing new revelations to me daily. I know I'm airing some dirty laundry here, but I'm very human. Can I blame my mother? She raised me. Ok, I won't blame her. Oh and by the way I had a great mom that let me be a free spirit, which kept me in a lot of trouble.*

Oftentimes we know how to act as Christians but fail to act as God intended us to act. *In other words, we let our tongues loose, and they get us into a lot of trouble. God is in us, so wake up, and don't use hurtful words. Watch what you say to those that are part of your life. If it's not a positive word, don't say it.*

Love never fails if we are in Christ.

For all of us to be successful in our Christian life, we have to make up our mind to do what the Word says. Living each day for Him will bring you into the spiritual walk that you desire and long for.

Chapter 34

God's Perfect Timing

"By Denise Gale"

"Delight yourself in the Lord and He will give you the desire of your heart."

(Psalms 37:4 NIV)

I grew up in the best family. We were "that family" that went to church on Sunday morning, Sunday night, and Wednesday night. I couldn't have asked for a better home life or childhood. I had the best godly parents and an older sister that loved and adored me. She was my only sibling. Her name was Beth. She set the bar high for me because she was a hard act to follow. She was an A student, played the piano (of course hymns), memorized tons of Scripture, was kind and compassionate. She was the responsible one. I, on the other hand, loved having a good time and being silly. She would always be the first to laugh at one of my jokes. Sharing her heart was easy for her. She always told me she loved me—every day! I have always had a hard time being serious. It was easy to make people laugh—much easier than letting my guard down and letting them see my true feelings. When she would tell me she loved me, I would smile. Then she would smile because she knew that was my way of telling her I loved her too. This went on throughout our growing up. And grow up we did. She married and had three children. I married and had two children. Her family moved to Florida, and my family remained in Arkansas.

One January seventh, many years ago, my life changed with a phone call. I was at work when Beth called to wish me a happy anniversary. I had a heavy heart that day and began to tell her all my troubles. With her same kindness and compassion, she began to minister to me like she always had. And, of course, before we hung up she said, "Dee, I love you." That day I said it back. When we hung up my heart was full. I felt like I needed to write her a letter telling her just how much I loved her. I wanted to thank her for always being my biggest fan and loving me the way she did. So I did. I spent my lunch hour that day writing a three-page letter doing just that. For someone who didn't like sharing her heart, this was one serious letter. I mailed it on my way home from work that same day.

On January 18, just eleven days later, my brother-in-law called my parents with news that Beth had taken ill, very ill, and was in the hospital. He advised my dad that it was bad and that we needed to come *now*. My dad had a fear of flying, so my parents and I jumped in the car and headed to Florida. This was before cell-phones, so we would stop along the way to call from pay phones to check on her condition. We were about an hour away when my dad received the news that Beth had died.

What! How did something like Toxic shock syndrome take my sister from us at this young age? Why did this happen? She was twenty-nine years old. She had three children ages five, four, and eighteen months. She got sick on a Friday and died on a Monday. My parents began to weep uncontrollably. I was in shock. Up to this point, nothing bad had ever happened to me. When we arrived at Beth's house, her husband

and children had not arrived back home yet. The house was empty. Entering the front door, my mother fell to her knees screaming, "My baby, my baby!" My Dad fell into a chair weeping. My heart was breaking. How could this be happening? She had always been there for me. She was my biggest fan. She would know how to help my parents! She was the responsible, compassionate one. She was supposed to help bury my parents someday. I was *not* supposed to bury her!

Then the phone began to ring. I had never been to her home in Florida, so I didn't know where the phone was. Listening to the ringing, it led me to a phone in her bedroom right beside her bed. On the other end of the phone was my very best friend in the whole world. God knew I needed to talk to her. His timing is *always* perfect! As I hung up the phone, I looked down on Beth's bedside table. There was my letter. All three pages. Tear stained. You could tell they had been read several times.

I realized in that moment that God was in control and His timing was perfect. He knew how to get me in that bedroom by making the phone ring at just the right moment. He put the desire in my best friend's heart to call at just that moment. He gave me the desire to write that letter eleven days before this moment in time. He knew I couldn't have lived through this without knowing that Beth knew just how much I loved her.

As I could hear my parents weeping in the living room, I clutched those pages to my chest and began to cry. God and I shared a special moment. Oh, how I thanked Him for allowing me to tell her just how much I loved her before he called her home. I thanked Him for allowing me to be raised in a Christian home and taught how God could be trusted and that His timing was always perfect. I had the reassurance that I would see her again someday in heaven. I thanked Him that He picked her out of all the sisters in the world to be my big sister. I was grateful that I could rest in Him and trust His perfect timing in all of this.

> *"In their hearts humans plan their course, but the LORD establishes their steps."*
>
> (Proverbs 16:9 NIV)

> *"And my God will meet all your needs according to his glorious riches."*
>
> (Philippians 4:19 NIV)

This was one of the first times I remember being able to trace God's hand on my journey here on earth. But, wow, what a tracing! His timing is perfect and He can be trusted.

Chapter 35

A Vessel Fit for the Master's Use

In the Old Testament God gave Moses the instructions for the tabernacle. There were instructions for the vessels and utensils—there were those for the highest table entirely made of gold and then those for the low uses—and the altar for burnt offerings.

This is what the New Testament is telling us.

> *"However God's firm foundation stands, having this seal, "The Lord knows those who are His and, "Let everyone who names the name of the Lord depart from unrighteousness. "Now in a large house there are not only vessels of gold and of silver, but also of wood and of clay. Some are for honor, and some for dishonor. If anyone therefore purges himself from these, he will be a vessel for honor, sanctified, and suitable for the master's use, prepared for every good work."*
>
> (2 Timothy: 2:19–21 WEB)

What kind of vessel do we want to be? One fit and ready for the Master's use and for good work.

Who does the purging or cleaning of the vessel? Jesus has already done His part.

Paul wrote to Timothy, who was a Spirit-filled servant: "Cleanse yourself and separate yourself from the world."

And how do we cleanse ourselves?

Really take an honest look at yourself by going back and recalling what you said today to those that you love or work with. It's always good to think about how you can improve on your relationship with others and from that point on you'll be walking in the spirit and not in the flesh.

- Did I do anything that was not in line with God's Word that was not conformed to God's will?

- Did I say things that were displeasing to Him?

- Did I omit to do something He wanted me to do?

You need to be honest with yourself here.

1. Ask God to show you things.

2. Then ask forgiveness

3. Forget it then, and don't remind yourself what you fell short on.

4. Then take Communion, the Lord's Body and Blood

Bring about a healing balm to the things you've seen and done and been forgiven for. Once you give it to God, it will be a healing for your spirit and soul, and the things you've done are erased.

Jesus' body was broken for our healing. He took the beating for us by taking those thirty-nine strikes from the Roman guard who beat him, breaking His body.

As we partake of the bread, which represents His body, we become more like Him.

When we come to the Lord's Table to take Communion, Satan cannot condemn us for doing this in Jesus' memory.

Avoid contact with contaminating and corrupting influence. People can cause us to say things we don't want to say and lead us in the wrong direction from God.

Have nothing do with youthful lusts and desires.

Have nothing to do with trifling and stupid controversies, which foster and breed quarrels.

A vessel fit for the Master's work is one that:

1. Has cleansed himself
2. Pursues all that is good and right, living and conforming to God's Word
3. Is kind to everyone
4. Is mild-tempered

5. Has tamed his tongue
6. Preserves the bond of peace
7. Strives to do God's work
8. Relaxes in God so He can use you

Chapter 36

Pleasing God

Sacrifices need to be acceptable to God, vessels fit for the Master's use, pleasing to God.

A vessel of pure gold is soft and pliable. It is only when mixed with something else that the hardness comes in. As we set ourselves to please God, we relax in Him and let Him work in and through us.

> *"Therefore, since Christ suffered for us in the flesh, arm yourselves also with the same mind; for he who has suffered in the flesh has ceased from sin; that you no longer should live the rest of your time in the flesh for the lusts of men, but for the will of God."*
>
> (1 Peter 4:1–2)

Jesus suffered for each of us. He suffered rather than fail to please God. We need to stop worrying about pleasing ourselves and look to pleasing God.

We need to have the mind of Christ in us at all times, so we can please God the Father.

> "For those who live according to the flesh set their minds on the things of the flesh, but those who live according to the Spirit, the things of the Spirit. For the mind of the flesh is death, but the mind of the Spirit is life and peace; because the mind of the flesh is hostile toward God; for it is not subject to God's law, neither indeed can it be. Those who are in the flesh can't please God. But you are not in the flesh but in the Spirit, if it is so that the Spirit of God dwells in you. But if any man doesn't have the Spirit of Christ, he is not his If Christ is in you, the body is dead because of sin, but the spirit is alive because of righteousness. But if the Spirit of him who raised up Jesus from the dead dwells in you, he who raised up Christ Jesus from the dead will also give life to your mortal bodies through his Spirit who dwells in you."
>
> (Romans 8:5–11 ESV)

One who is pleasing to God does not let his mind dictate and control his five senses but lets the Holy Spirit direct and control every part of his life.

Renew your mind. Your mind should be thinking the way God's Word says.

Do not be moved by people and what they say.

Do not be moved by your thoughts in your mind but by the Word of God.

> "Without faith it is impossible to be well pleasing to him, for he who comes to God must believe that he exists, and that he is a rewarded of those who seek him."
>
> (Hebrews 11:6 WEB)

Faith pleases God. He has given us His faith. We still have control of our own wills, but we still need to follow the guidance of the Holy Spirit.

Pleasing God

Faith is relying on or trusting confidently in our Father.

When we let our minds get in the way, we are not pleasing God.

When I think I feel a certain way, this involves the mind. But when we turn this off and stand on God's Word, we can grow in faith.

> *"Have this in your mind, which was also in Christ Jesus, who, existing in the form of God, didn't consider equality with God a thing to be grasped, but emptied himself, taking the form of a servant, being made in the likeness of men. And being found in human form, he humbled himself, becoming obedient to death, yes, the death of the cross. Therefore God also highly exalted him, and gave to him the name which is above every name; that at the name of Jesus every knee should bow, of those in heaven, those on earth, and those under the earth, and that every tongue should confess that Jesus Christ is Lord, to the glory of God the Father."*
>
> *"So then, my beloved, even as you have always obeyed, not only in my presence, but now much more in my absence, work out your own salvation with fear and trembling. For it is God who works in you both to will and to work, for his good pleasure."*
>
> (Philippians 2:5–13 WEB)

The mind of Christ is in us. It is God working His will in us that changes us so we can enter into His presence and have the same mind of Christ.

> *"Therefore, with minds that are alert and fully sober, set your hope on the grace to be brought to you when Jesus Christ is revealed at his coming. As obedient children, do not conform to the evil desires you had when you lived in ignorance. But just as he who called you is holy, so be holy in all you do; for it is written: "Be holy, because I am holy."*

> *"Since you call on a Father who judges each person's work impartially, live out your time as foreigners here in reverent fear."*
>
> (1 Peter 1:13–17 NIV)

Brace up our mind in Him. The brace is the Word of God. This pleases our Father.

Be holy as our Father is holy. Pleasing Him is obedience to His Word.

Jesus always did that which was pleasing to His father.

> *"But if anyone obeys his word, love for God is truly made complete in them. This is how we know we are in him: Whoever claims to live in him must live as Jesus did."*
>
> (1 John 2:5–6 WEB)

Jesus conformed to the will of His Father in every purpose, thought, and action.

> *"Whoever claims to live in him must live as Jesus did."*
>
> (1 John 2:6 NIV)

Jesus' purpose or reason for coming was to redeem and save the world.

> *"Jesus said, "I can of myself do nothing. As I hear, I judge, and my judgment is righteous; because I don't seek my own will, but the will of my Father who sent me."*
>
> (John 5:30)

> *"The thief only comes to steal, kill, and destroy. I came that they may have life, and may have it abundantly. I am the good shepherd. The good*

> *shepherd lays down his life for the sheep. He who is a hired hand, and not a shepherd, who doesn't own the sheep, sees the wolf coming, leaves the sheep, and flees. The wolf snatches the sheep, and scatters them. The hired hand flees because he is a hired hand, and doesn't care for the sheep. I am the good shepherd. I know my own, and I'm known by my own; even as the Father knows me, and I know the Father. I lay down my life for the sheep."*
>
> (John 10:10–12 WEB)

Jesus pleased his Father in every way.

> *"Him who knew no sin he made* to be *sin on our behalf; that we might become the righteousness of God in him."*
>
> (2 Corinthians 5:21 NIV)

We are to fulfill God's purpose or His will in our lives. Let God take over every aspect of your life. This includes who we marry.

Women are to fulfill their role as helpmeets and encourage. *I think as men we should do the same and encourage and support our wives. If we don't meet in the middle and support each other it's hard for us to love each other and get anything accomplished as a couple.*

We should lead others to God by sharing Jesus. We need to have a ministry of reconciliation.

As Christians we are to reconcile with anyone that we feel we have offended.

We should also help others end any conflicts they have with others in their own lives, so they can renew and rebuild friendships with their family and friends.

Working toward a fellowship with our Heavenly Father will keep us on the right track.

> *"But if we walk in the light, as he is in the light, we have fellowship with one another, and the blood of Jesus Christ, his Son, cleanses us from all sin."*
>
> (1 John 3:7 WEB)

Jesus' thoughts were to accomplish that which was pleasing to His Father.

> *"I don't receive glory from men. But I know you that you don't have God's love in yourselves. I have come in my Father's name, and you don't receive me. If another comes in his own name, you will receive him. How can you believe, who receive glory from one another, and you don't seek the glory that comes from the only God?"*
>
> (John 5:41–44 WEB)

Our thought should be to conform to God's will and obey His every commandment.

> *"But whoever keeps his word, God's love has most certainly been perfected in him. This is how we know that we are in him: he who says he remains in him ought himself also to walk just like he walked."*
>
> (1 John 2:5–6 WEB)

We are to walk like our Savior did and conduct ourselves as He did.

> *"Finally, brothers, whatever things are true, whatever things are honorable, whatever things are just, whatever things are pure, whatever things are lovely, whatever things are of good report; if there is any virtue, and if there is any praise, think about these things."*
>
> (Philippians 4:8 WEB)

Pleasing God

> *"Jesus therefore answered them, "Most certainly, I tell you, the Son can do nothing of himself, but what he sees the Father doing. For whatever things he does these the Son also does likewise."*
>
> (John 5:19 WEB)

Jesus' actions were the actions of His Father. *And so should ours be.*

> *"Do not merely listen to the word, and so deceive yourselves. Do what it says."*
>
> (James 1:22 NIV)

We must be doers of the Word as He was. We must do whatever God's Word says we are to do. We cannot please God without faith.

> *"For this is loving God, that we keep his commandments. His commandments are not grievous. For whatever is born of God overcomes the world. This is the victory that has overcome the world: your faith."*
>
> (1 John 5:3–4 WEB)

We need to keep the precepts. *A precept is a principle that we should guide our life by and will guide our moral behavior.*

> *"Without faith it is impossible to be well pleasing to him, for he who comes to God must believe that he exists, and that he is a rewarder of those who seek him."*
>
> (Hebrews 11:6 WEB)

> *"For whatever is born of God overcomes the world. This is the victory that has overcome the world: your faith. Who is he who overcomes the world, but he who believes that Jesus is the Son of God?"*
>
> (1 John 5:4–5 NIV)

Faith is our victory!

Chapter 37

Children

God first loved us—loved us so much that He gave His only begotten Son for us. We can live such lives before our children and share with them that they will be led to Christ.

One thing Juanita wanted to do is teach small children about God's love and how to become a Christian. She taught small children at Agape church in Little Rock for years and believed that even the youngest of children would be able to retain what she taught them. She believed if they heard the Word of God, it would get in their spirits and it would be there a lifetime. And I can testify that this happened when she was teaching those children.

"If I speak with the languages of men and of angels, but don't have love, I have become sounding brass, or a clanging cymbal. If I have the gift of prophecy, and know all mysteries and all knowledge; and if I have all faith, so as to remove mountains, but don't have love, I am nothing. If I dole out all my goods to feed the poor, and if I give my body to be burned, but don't have love, it profits me nothing."

"Love is patient and is kind; love doesn't envy. Love doesn't brag, is not proud, doesn't behave itself inappropriately, doesn't seek its own way, is not provoked, takes no account of evil; doesn't rejoice in

unrighteousness, but rejoices with the truth; bears all things, believes all things, hopes all things, endures all things. Love never fails. But where there are prophecies, they will be done away with. Where there are various languages, they will cease. Where there is knowledge, it will be done away with."

(1 Corinthians 13:1–8 WEB)

- God is patient and endures long. How patient are we with our children? Just stop and think of how God endured for many years and was patient with us as we stumbled along without even thinking about Him.

- God is not boastful or arrogant and is not inflated with pride. Do we treat our children with an attitude of "we know it all" or a "look at me, I've really got it together" attitude? And all the time in our hearts we are judging them.

- God is not rude and does not act unbecoming. Are we treating our friends with more courtesy than we do our children? We tell their secrets without thinking. God keeps us in confidence.

- God does not insist on His own rights or own way. How fretful have you been with your children lately?

- God takes no account of the evil done Him—He loves us. He pays no attention to a wrong suffered. How many years were we rebellious children to our Father or just plain lazy, idle children? When we were children, we didn't pay attention to what our Father wanted us to do, and He loved us anyway. But then we get uptight when our children say something about us or to us. Instead we should learn to register no emotions other than love in all things.

Children

- Love bears up under anything or any circumstances

- Love is ever ready to believe the best. God believes the best in us. We, on the other hand, are ready to be suspicious, knowing that our children are going to do something bad and are expecting the worst. We're going to get what we expect, good or bad. Believe the best—expect the best—from your children.

- Love never fails to soften a belligerent attitude. That's the way God got us—He loved us. We can love people and our family into the kingdom of God.

- Love forgives. We say we forgive our children—but we don't because we keep bringing it up to them or remembering it.

"Whenever you stand praying, forgive, if you have anything against anyone; so that your Father, who is in heaven, may also forgive you your transgressions. But if you do not forgive, neither will your Father in heaven forgive your transgressions."

(Mark 11:25–26 WEB)

God listens to us. How many years was it that we didn't talk to our Father? He never gave up on us. Commit your children to the Lord, love them, and listen to the Lord for wisdom to guide them. Don't take them back from the Lord.

"Therefore prepare your minds for action, be sober, and set your hope fully on the grace that will be brought to you at the revelation of Jesus Christ—as children of obedience, not conforming yourselves according to your former lusts as in your ignorance, but just as he who called you is holy, you yourselves also be holy in all of your behavior; because it is

written, "You shall be holy; for I am holy." If you call on him as Father, who without respect of persons judges according to each man's work, pass the time of your living as foreigners here in reverent fear."

(1 Peter 1:13–17 WEB)

"Therefore, beloved, seeing that you look for these things, be diligent to be found in peace, without defect and blameless in his sight."

(2 Peter 3:14 WEB)

"Don't judge, so that you won't be judged. For with whatever judgment you judge, you will be judged; and with whatever measure you measure, it will be measured to you. Why do you see the speck that is in your brother's eye, but don't consider the beam that is in your own eye? Or how will you tell your brother, 'Let me remove the speck from your eye;' and behold, the beam is in your own eye?"

(Matthew 7:1–5 WEB)

What does it mean to be without spot or blemish before the Lord?

1. Be lined up with His will and His Word

2. What are some areas that we need to be lined up in?

3. Judge not—Jesus is the Judge, not us.

4. Never provoke your children to wrath.

"You fathers, don't provoke your children to wrath, but nurture them in the discipline and instruction of the Lord."

(Ephesians 6:4 WEB)

5. Examine yourselves daily to see if you are walking in the Spirit and not in the flesh.

6. Take the Lord's Supper.

7. Be obedient in all areas.

8. Don't talk about or criticize others.

Juanita and Dudley taught little children for years and believed that as parents we need to teach them these same principles of Christianity, so they can become Christ like.

She took time to listen and knew that without little children to mold into God's army, who would fight the fight against the spiritual forces that try daily to take down every generation that is born into this world? If you don't fully understand what is occurring, you might want to look at the world that you live in.

Chapter 38

Charlee's Faith

"By Russell Morrison"

I have wanted to write about my daughter's faith for many years, but putting her story on paper has been a very hard thing for me to do. It most likely will rip my heart out while writing each word down.

My wife, Patti, and I both just wanted to raise a family and enjoy the American dream. We both worked very hard to provide a good home for our kids, and we both worked extra to make it so. We had one son, Denton, and our daughter, Charlee Diane.

We rocked along raising our kids for about thirteen years before the storm hit. Patti had one of worst accidents anyone could ever have. She had a head-on collision with a large truck. This wreck just about caused her death. Our family kept on praying for a miracle, and it happened. After a few hours of surgery, Patti made it through one of the biggest hurdles our young family had to get through. Her face, arms, and feet had been cut up badly. I didn't have any idea what would happen to us next.

After a few weeks, we could not believe how much better Patti was doing, although we both knew it would take a few years to recover fully. But she kept on going. Two weeks after her accident, we were invited to a friend's house for dinner.

After dinner my wife said that I should check on my mother who lived just a mile or so away. When we drove over to check on my mother, I saw a coroner's car in her driveway. My mother had passed away at the early age of fifty-two. It seemed that the world was falling apart around us, that it had come to our home to test our faith, and that it was trying to rock the very core of who we were as Christians.

Once my wife was better, life started really throwing hard balls my way and all I could do was to keep up my faith and keep going on with whatever came my way. The next big disaster came at my daughter's birthday party, when she was thirteen. This one hit us like a ton of Malvern bricks. (If you're wondering there is a brick making facility in Malvern, Arkansas)

My wife Patti hired a Christian band to play for Charlee's birthday party, and we had invited a lot of her friends and Patti's parents, Juanita and Dudley. During the party, Charlee came up to me and said she had a terrible headache and did not feel well. Her grandfather took a look at her and noticed that she had little red spots on her. Later we found out these are called petechiae ("pet-TEA-key-eye"). Petechiae are tiny, flat red or purple spots in the skin or the lining of the mouth caused by abnormal bleeding from small blood vessels that have broken close to the skin or the surface of a mucous membrane. They can spread over a large area of the body within a few hours. The spots range from pinpoint-size to BB-size and do not itch or cause pain. They are different than most little red spots. They do not turn white when a person presses on them. When petechiae develop quickly over a few hours, it may mean that a serious infection or a lack of platelets (part of the body's defense against bleeding) has developed and requires immediate medical treatment.

Once her grandfather had noticed the red spots, he said, "Take her to the hospital now." He must have had an idea something was very wrong. We called the party off and headed for the Benton hospital.

The hospital did not want to keep her, thinking it was an allergic reaction to aspirin. Patti explained that her dad was a pharmacist and that he had thought it was very important to really check her out. They did a blood test and found out that her white count was through the roof. After admitting her for the night, they sent us to Arkansas Children's Hospital in Little Rock. Once they released us from the Benton hospital, I drove her to Children's Hospital, putting on my flashers, I drove a little too fast from the fear of the unknown.

At Children's they went into action and took blood samples. Two days later she had a very tough bone marrow test that hurt her so much I could hardly bear seeing her in this type of pain. Charlee was my baby girl, and this hurt like no other pain I have ever felt. Growing up in the world I grew up in, I knew pain in many forms, and this pain was something I will never be able to describe.

The doctors told us she had an adult leukemia. I went into her room and told her the very bad news with tears in my eyes. She told me not to worry—that a friend of hers at our local church had made it just fine going through the ordeal of a brain tumor. She told me she would be just fine. Right then and there I knew my little girl of ninety-five pounds would be fine. I knew that she trusted in God, and that's all that mattered to me at that moment.

The next day the leukemia fight started. Into ICU we went and didn't come out of the hospital for the next few months. The first night in ICU was so intense that our baby girl was about to die as the enlarged white cells tried to pass through the blood vessels in her brain. As we stood back and watched and didn't even know how to pray, God had it covered. It was three in the morning when the chemo began to work and things begin to change. The next morning at least five people called to say that God woke them up at three in the morning to pray for Charlee and was she OK? These were people in different states and cities all around, who had no way of knowing how sick she had been. Thank God for our many friends and family that took time out to pray and give us the needed support to make it through this fight that must have come straight from hell.

I had never seen a group of doctors and nursing staff take on such a life-and-death situation in my life. They had a charting table and two nurses that took care of the medications and a nurse to keep up with the many IV pumps. I would say that those were some of the finest nurses in this part of the world.

Through many hours of prayers and God's guidance of the medical team, Charlee came out of the ICU to continue a battle for her life that we thought we would never get through. After a few months, she was in remission from this life-threatening beast. She did lose all of her hair going through this first battle, but she never gave up the fight.

The day we came home from the hospital was a great day for our family. Charlee had lost weight and her hair, but her drive to live was like no other. She was in remission from the leukemia that just about took her life, and that was a miracle from God.

Charlee's Faith

She was a very weak girl when she came home, but she still continued to have a great outlook on a very tough situation. Her faith seemed to kick in. She knew that her friend Amber who had cancer, survived so she could too. I had never seen a young person like Charlee be so brave. I would have been a basket case with what she had just gone through. She had been in the hospital going through some of the worst things that you can imagine.

During this time I kept a journal of what was happening to Charlee and my entire family and kept it going for many years. I would write down when she went into the hospital and even the fun times that she and her brother were having. Even though life was really going down the tubes, we still tried to have some type of family life. I remember taking Charlee to ride the go-karts. As a young and dumb dad, I didn't think that her blood count could be low, but most likely thought, well, if the cancer could possibly take her life, let's still enjoy every day that we had. She had a blast riding the go-karts that day.

A few months went by, and the cancer came back. This time it did not appear that she would come out of this one alive. Once she came out of the ICU, it was time to find a bone marrow donor. A young lady in the military was a perfect match. We were ecstatic that a perfect match was found. She had her bone marrow transplant at 1:30 a.m. at the Med Center. We had some of our closest friends there to cheer her on and pray over the bone marrow before it went into her body: Bill Howard, our pastor, along with Joe Nance and Bob Wellborn. What a dedicated group of men praying for a young girl to survive a disease that was trying to take her life.

Charlee was out of the hospital on October 18, another good day for her and our family, but we were just about worn out. My wife and I had spent many nights and weekends trying to give our daughter the support that she needed, but we were both in a cloud of despair. One wonderful thing is that God kept sending people to encourage us and Charlee as we traveled through this chapter in our lives with only our faith and the hope of a miracle to bring us through.

One thing I do remember that really seemed to help Charlee get through this horrible ordeal was when an entire team of pep-stepper girls came out from school in a bus. All the girls swam and had a wonderful day cheering Charlee up. What a great day of fun.

It was the same way when she was in the hospital. On many occasions the nurses would just let us have fun. The nurses in the bone marrow unit at Children's Hospital were from all over the world, and I thought that was pretty cool. One night Charlee was really sick from throwing up—going through day after day of chemo and radiation would just make her sick as a dog. The nurse let me bring my fiddle into the unit, and before you knew it, these nurses from Ireland and Scotland were dancing and having a marvelous time.

Our Charlee sat up in the bed and laughed until she almost cried. Little things like this helped bring us back to a normal life, and those nurses were helping all of us let off some steam. Praise God for the caring nurses and doctors at Arkansas Children's Hospital who helped bring back so many sick children to a normal life again. I will never forget them and the respiratory therapist, Ken, who worked with the RT team. They really were outstanding and always gave us hope.

Later as a patient at UAMS in Little Rock, she had a bone marrow transplant and continued to receive IV medications and chemo on an outpatient basis. There she met other patients who were from all over the

Charlee's Faith

World. One day she revealed to us that she believed that God wanted her right where she was at, not that he made her sick, but that he allowed her to be on this mission field, where she could share her faith with others. She believed that with all her heart and share she did!

Well, Charlee's faith was challenged each day for many years, but she kept on going until she was twenty-one years of age. She was in her senior year of college at Ouachita Baptist and home to visit for a weekend when she fell in the driveway as my wife and daughter-in-law were taking her to see the doctor. She told her mother to call 911—she knew she was going to pass out. The ambulance came and took her to our small-town hospital where she stayed for a week and then was transported to the med center in Little Rock. She was diagnosed with acute liver failure. While in the Benton hospital, she wrote a note to us that she knew she would not be coming home. After passing a few notes we all realized that she was not ever coming home. At that point in my life, all I could do was trust in God.

After many years of her struggle, Patti asked her if she would have gone through all the chemo and bone marrow transplant and being sick for years if she had to do it over again. She said that without a doubt she would. I will never forget knowing that I had a child who never gave up on her faith and fought like a lion through the trying life that she had. It is a true honor to have been her dad. Life keeps throwing lemons at us, it seems, but when that happens, all you can do is make lemonade—and she did.

Although it looked like Charlee had lost her battle with cancer, she had not; Charlee received the ultimate healing, to be with Jesus!

I love you, Charlee

Chapter 39

Faith

I found wonderful notes on faith in one of my daughter's journals. It started with this Scripture in Hebrews.

"But the righteous will live by faith."
(Hebrews 10:38 WEB)

The just shall live by faith, and I have seen those so close to me live each and every day like it was going to be their last.

My daughter Charlee passed away when she was twenty-one years of age, and the one thing that kept her alive for eight more years after she was diagnosed with leukemia at age thirteen was her strong faith in God.

Her grandmother Juanita lived a life of faith as well and taught her one thing: that she was to never give up and to put all your trust in God. I really didn't think that my daughter had such a strong faith like Juanita, but she did and then some. Both these women never gave up on life or their faith in God. It was a knockout punch that took both of them out of this world. And when it comes my time, I hope I can hold on to the same faith as they did.

What is faith?

Abraham called things as though they were. He trusted God and believed what He said to him—that he would be the father of nations...*and he was.*

> *"Looking to Jesus, the author and perfecter of faith, who for the joy that was set before him endured the cross, despising its shame, and has sat down at the right hand of the throne of God."*
>
> (Hebrews 12:2 KJV)

Jesus is the author and finisher of our faith. Jesus is the utmost in our faith. He completely and totally believes His Father. He spoke what His Father said and did what His Father said to do.

What does it mean the just shall live by faith? How do we get faith?

> *"For I say, through the grace that was given me, to every man who is among you, not to think of himself more highly than he ought to think; but to think reasonably, as God has apportioned to each person a measure of faith."*
>
> (Romans 12:3 WEB)

God gives to each believer the same measure of faith. We just have to believe and trust him.

> *So faith comes by hearing, and hearing by the word of God.*
>
> (Roman 10:17 WEB)

Have you noticed in your life that every time you think about studying God's Word/Bible something seems to come up and you don't have the time to study or even listen to someone share the gospel? What is going on with that? I believe that

Faith

we are fighting a spiritual warfare each day, and something out there does not want us to study and to know who God really is.

A hindrance to our faith is the lack of knowledge of God's Word. It seems like there are so many things that keep us from just taking a few minutes a day to study and pray. There are so many out there that are truly disciplined and take time out of each day to study and pray.

> "Jesus answered them, "Have faith in God. For most certainly I tell you, whoever may tell this mountain, 'Be taken up and cast into the sea,' and doesn't doubt in his heart, but believes that what he says is happening; he shall have whatever he says. Therefore I tell you, all things whatever you pray and ask for, believe that you have received them, and you shall have them. Whenever you stand praying, forgive, if you have anything against anyone; so that your Father, who is in heaven, may also forgive you your transgressions. But if you do not forgive, neither will your Father in heaven forgive your transgressions."
>
> (Mark 11:22–26)

Have faith in God.

> "In Lystra there sat a man who was lame. He had been that way from birth and had never walked. He listened to Paul as he was speaking. Paul looked directly at him, saw that he had faith to be healed and called out, "Stand up on your feet!" At that, the man jumped up and began to walk. The man heard Paul preaching and acted on it with his faith got up with a leap and walked."
>
> (Acts 14:8–10 NIV)

> "Whatever is not of faith is sin."
>
> (Romans 14:23)

What is the difference between "mental assent" and faith? Mental assent agrees with the mind but never acts on God's Word.

> *"My son, attend to my words. Turn your ear to my sayings. Let them not depart from your eyes. Keep them in the center of your heart. For they are life to those who find them and health to their whole body."*
>
> (Proverbs 4:20–22)

Medicine to all flesh is what the Word of God is.

"Attend to My words." Believe God's Word, and act on it.

Jesus is the author and finisher of our faith.

> *"Having then a great high priest, who has passed through the heavens, Jesus, the Son of God, let us hold tightly to our confession."*
>
> (Hebrews 4:14)

Hold fast to our confession regarding whatever you are believing God for. God does not lie. His word is true. He stands behind it and is quick to perform it.

> *"Then said Jehovah unto me, Thou hast well seen: for I watch over my word to perform it."*
>
> (Jeremiah 1:12)

> *"For we walk by faith, not by sight."*
>
> (2 Corinthians 5:7)

There are many intervals in our lives that we have to trust in God to get us through tough situations. I remember Juanita praying for something as simple as

Faith

a parking place when she was out doing her shopping or taking care of any business. I watched her on many occasions pray for the very sick and she truly believed in her heart they would be healed. She would put her faith into overdrive and would not let doubt come into the situation to interfere with her faith.

My wife, Patti, and her cousin Rita were on a road trip in the state of Washington a year ago. They were in a very remote area of Washington and were just about to run out of gas. Rita mentioned to Patti that they might want to say a prayer for gas because there were no gas stations within miles. Juanita had taught her daughter to trust in God for all your needs and to trust your faith. After a short prayer and about thirty miles or so down the road, they came up on a co-op gas station. They pulled in and at the same time a lady drove up to gas up. These types of gas stations are for co-op members only, and my wife explained to the lady that they were miles from the nearest gas station and needed help. The lady used her card to help my wife and cousin get the needed gas so they could finish their trip.

Was this just a random occurrence, or did Patti and Rita's faith kick in? I'm a believer, so, yes; I would say it was God's divine help that took care of their needs. After a few months at home following the Washington trip, my wife received an unexpected call from Rita, who said the same thing had happened to her again! She and her husband were traveling in a very remote part of Washington State and were just about to run out of gas again.

Rita said, "I really wonder if your prayers would work for a second time." Well, the two prayed for a little help, and running on fumes she arrived at a gas station. Rita was again pleasantly surprised. I'm not saying that every time you ask God for a new car you will receive one or even when your health has started failing that you will get the answer you want. You don't get everything you pray for all the time. But I do believe we need to trust God and rely on Him for all our needs. I think we just need to trust God in everything we do and have faith as a simple child for Him to take care of all our needs.

Juanita's Gift

I mentioned earlier the horrible car accident that just about took Patti's life in 1987—that was a day I will never forget. When Patti was brought to Doctors Hospital by ambulance and taken back into surgery she stopped the doctors and asked them if she could pray for them before they began the surgery. She prayed that God would guide their hands as they performed the operation. I think this simple prayer of faith really touched the doctors who were just trying to save her life. They were stunned to think she wanted to pray that God would guide their hands as they performed the delicate procedures to put her back together again. I found out that day that Juanita had left an imprint of faith on this young woman who was now my wife. Nothing was going to challenge that faith that her mother had instilled in her. And at that particular time I was very glad she had that type of faith to trust God even when all the odds were against her. This is what I call faith!

> *"Now that no man is justified by the law before God is evident: for "The righteous shall live by faith."*
>
> (Galatians 3:11)

> *"Yes, a man will say, "You have faith, and I have works." Show me your faith without works, and I by my works will show you my faith. Faith without works is dead."*
>
> (James 2:18, 19)

What prevents us so often from reaching that faith plateau where we can move mountains? When we are thinking wrong and believing wrong. God's Word is given to us to get our thinking back in line with His.

Chapter 40

Fruit of Our Lips

God in the beginning created all things. He spoke it into being. God is still creating.

> "For I, Jehovah, change not; therefore ye, O sons of Jacob, are not consumed."
>
> (Malachi 3:6)

God does not change who He is or how he feels about us.

> "Jesus Christ is the same yesterday, today, and forever."
>
> (Hebrews 13:8)

> "I create the fruit of the lips: Peace, peace, to him that is far off and to him that is near, saith Jehovah; and I will heal him."
>
> (Isaiah 57:19)

> "Through him, then, let us offer up a sacrifice of praise to God continually, that is, the fruit of lips which proclaim allegiance to his name. But don't forget to be doing good and sharing, for with such sacrifices God is well pleased."
>
> (Hebrews 13:15)

How do we tap into God's power to meet our needs? We need to ask God for the things that we need.

> *"Therefore I tell you, all things whatever you pray and ask for, believe that you have received them, and you shall have them."*
>
> (Mark 11:23)

As we confess God's Word, it begins to create a new life in every word that comes out of our mouths.

Man is the only created being that can talk and can utter words.

> *"I form the light, and create darkness; I make peace, and create evil. I am Jehovah, that doeth all these things."*
>
> (Isaiah 45:7)

God said, "I create the fruits of our lips; if it is good or evil."

We also can control what flows out of our mouths.

What flows out of our mouths can be positive or negative. It can hurt or cause wonderful things to happen to us and those around us.

What we say to our spouses or to our children or even our coworkers can create a hell or heaven in our homes and work places. What can we do to make life better for our families, friends, and coworkers? I hope you take time to say things that will cause life and not death. I can remember words that people say to me many years after they were said. If I say something that hurts someone, I remember what I said for years later. I want to say the right things and want to make sure it will not hurt the others in a way that will cause them pain. Words can bring life or death.

Fruit of Our Lips

God says, "I will give you the desires of your heart." Desire His Word and begin to speak it.

> *"You are trapped by the words of your mouth. You are ensnared with the words of your mouth."*
>
> (Proverbs 6:2 NIV)

If you say you won't ever be successful, most likely you won't have those things in life you want and need. I do believe if you are constantly saying negative things then that is what will come your way. Be positive about everything that comes out of your mouth. Juanita would on many occasions say, "You can have everything you believe in." Trust in your faith; believe that God can make it happen. Ten years ago my wife called me at work and said she had found the perfect house for us. It was in town and had wonderful potential. Well she called her mother and I drove down from Little Rock and took a look at the house. Oh my, I just had to have it and asked Juanita to say one of her wonderful powerful prayers. I said Juanita pray with me about this house and she said let's do it now. She said where two or more agree in the name of Jesus it would happen. Yes, within a few days, we had bought the house and were moved in within a week. God does take care of us, just take time to believe.

> *"My son, attend to my words. Turn your ear to my sayings. Let them not depart from your eyes. Keep them in the center of your heart. For they are life to those who find them, and health to their whole body. Keep your heart with all diligence, for out of it is the wellspring of life. Put away from yourself a perverse mouth. Put corrupt lips far from you. Let your eyes look straight ahead. Fix your gaze directly before you."*
>
> (Proverbs 4:20–25 WEB)

Controlling what you say is the key to being successful in every part of your life. I have worked in many places, and those people who didn't control what they said to others would be sure to fail in a short period of time and were looking for a new place to work. Just a little common sense will keep you in the work force.

> *"You offspring of vipers, how can you, being evil, speak good things? For out of the abundance of the heart, the mouth speaks The good man out of his good treasure brings out good things, and the evil man out of his evil treasure brings out evil things tell you that every idle word that men speak, they will give account of it in the day of judgment. For by your words you will be justified, and by your words you will be condemned."*
>
> Matthew 12:34–37 WEB)

The things that are in your heart will come out of your mouth, so watch out and control your tongue.

> *They triumphed over him by the blood of the Lamb and by the word of their testimony; they did not love their lives so much as to shrink from death.*
>
> (Revelation 12:11 NIV)

We can overcome the enemy by the word of our testimony. The secret of our faith is continually saying the Word of God. God's Word is truth and is healing to our bodies. Meditate on God's Word day and night. Put God's Word first, and place it in your hearts.

> *"If you remain in me, and my words remain in you, you will ask whatever you desire, and it will be done for you."*
>
> (John 15:7 WEB)

Once we open up to God's Word and truly start using the principals of our faith, it will change who you are and amazing things will start to happen.

Fruit of Our Lips

"Take words with you and return to the Lord. Say to him: "Forgive all our sins and receive us graciously, that we may offer the fruit of our lips."

(Hosea 14:2 NIV)

"Not many of you should become teachers, my fellow believers, because you know that we who teach will be judged more strictly. We all stumble in many ways. Anyone who is never at fault in what they say is perfect, able to keep their whole body in check."

"When we put bits into the mouths of horses to make them obey us, we can turn the whole animal. Or take ships as an example. Although they are so large and are driven by strong winds, they are steered by a very small rudder wherever the pilot wants to go. Likewise, the tongue is a small part of the body, but it makes great boasts. Consider what a great forest is set on fire by a small spark. The tongue also is a fire, a world of evil among the parts of the body. It corrupts the whole body, sets the whole course of one's life on fire, and is itself set on fire by hell."

(James 3: 1–6 NIV)

Chapter 41

Greater Health God's Way

There are several steps we need to take to have a peaceful living and reduce stress in our lives.

Stress is the response of the mind, emotion, and body to whatever demands are being made upon me.

Are we prepared to respond to stress each day? *Here lately I have not done so well with dealing with stress that has comes into my daily life. I asked my wife Patti to pray for me the other day about a few things that were driving me crazy and within the same day God came to my rescue. Wow! God is so good.*

Positive stress is happy, good, desirable, controllable, easy to cope with, pleasantly resolvable, and exciting. Some examples of good stress are when you complete a project that you start or when you have applied for a loan and it comes through. *Richard Carnahan, one of the men I work with has told me on many occasions, Russell, when you retire the lack of stress will kill you. There is stress in our lives and we need to learn how to deal with it to determine the outcomes. When stress is causing my body some major grief, I know that I have to give it to God.*

Negative stress is sad, maddening, disturbing, uncontrollable, un-resolvable, and depressing. Examples of negative stress are arguments with your spouse and getting a traffic ticket.

Negative stress takes the greatest toll on our bodies. My wife and I both were put under a tremendous amount of stress when our daughter was diagnosed with leukemia. Both of us were challenged each and every day with the stress of wondering if our daughter could continue to fight this horrible struggle just to stay alive. This stress went on for more than a decade until it took my young daughter's life. Going through those very trying days just about wrecked our bodies physically. We are still here even though negative stress tried to take us out. It weathered us and caused us a few health problems, but we are still here fighting the fight of faith.

We don't have to absorb negative stress into ourselves. We can decide each day that we will not allow stress in our lives. You really have to walk in faith to keep these various stress occurrences from being absorbed into your spirit and body. It is not good to allow our bodies to get sick by not controlling stress around us. We can control how we react to stress.

Some sources of stress

- Environment—this includes city living, with the noise and even the people that you live around.

- Poor diet—coffee, tea, sugar, white flour, salt, highly processed foods with chemical additives. *I think I'm in a little trouble on this one. I think this chapter is speaking to me!*

- Lack of exercise—physical exercise can minimize stress.

- Your attitude—how you react to a situation.

Signs of stress

Tenseness, irritability, depression, constant fatigue, the appearance of being in another world, forgetfulness, low tolerance of frustration, lack of patience, loss of appetite, sleeplessness, frequent headaches, sudden crying over minor things, allergic reaction, constipation, muscular aches and pains, skin ailment, high blood pressure, colitis, heart disease, cancer, ulcers. *I guess this chapter was meant for me.*

Some ways we can deal with stress

- Do something to change the situation in your life.

- Be content whatever the circumstance, and fortify yourself physically, mentally, and spiritually to survive it.

- Jesus is our source of peace.

- Be filled with the Holy Spirit.

- Spend time each day with God.

- Pray for all those around you.

- Praise God each day.

- Feed on God's Word daily.

- Confess God's Word out loud daily.

- Don't worry about things that can make you sick.

- Laugh—a merry heart doeth good like a medicine. *I would not make it without my daily laugh. I had a young boss about fourteen years ago who told me, "Russell, for me and you to have a good working relationship you're going to have to get serious." I think his humor must have been surgically removed because he sure did not have a sense of humor. He said I don't know if you're being funny or if it's a serious situation that I need to pay attention too. I told him I would work on it. I don't think we have to be serious all the time; I still have a little fun while I work.*

- Crying sometimes releases stress. *Putting a few stories in this book has caused me a few tears. I can say mostly tears of joy.*

To live truly in peace, we have to watch what comes out of our mouth. For out of the overflow of the heart the mouth speaks. What we say can either bring life to us or a situation, or it can bring death. Because we are made in the image of God, He gives us creative power to speak our world into existence too. We can have a world of disharmony, strife, suspicion, and hatred just by speaking a few words of death into a situation.

Keeping any anger inside of you and not forgiving is one of the most devastating ways to bring on stress, and all of the negative emotions it brings on can even cause us to get sick.

Jesus is our deliverer of feelings of inferiority and other childhood troubles. We are to be what God created us to be.

Doing a job that you don't enjoy can be very stressful and cause you to lose your peace. I will never find total health, total peace, or total anything in life if I'm working against what I was created to be or what God wanted me to do.

God has placed a high calling on my life. When we love doing something, we can find time for it.

Calmness and strength are lost in too much busyness and rush. In quietness and trust is your strength.

Get rid of things you can live without so you can better care for those that you love. Simplicity will bring peace into your life.

Stress is relieved by a right relationship with God, eating food the way God made it, physical exercise, drinking plenty of pure water, fasting, getting enough fresh air and sunshine, and rest. In other words, eat right and take care of yourselves. *I have not been a good steward of my body. My mother-in-law lived to be eighty-three and worked up to the last few weeks of her life. She worked at taking care of her temple. It's time for me take a walk.*

Chapter 42

Eleven Ways You Can Get Rid of Stress

How can we overcome stress in our daily lives? Most often stress comes from ourselves. We have feelings that we have a lack of time and money. Being stressed out makes us feel important. *Have you ever worked with someone who thought they were overworked? They seem to be going in circles and they never seem to get anything done. They work harder trying to get everyone around to believe they are just overworked.*

Martha in the Bible wanted everyone around her to know that she was important. She was the classic stressed-out person.

Too much stress can cause you a multitude of health problems such as fatigue, anxiety, low esteem, cancer, high blood pressure, and ulcers. Seventy-five to 90 percent of all visits to the doctor are from stress. Stress causes headaches, backache, irritability, forgetfulness, lack of sleep, and depression.

One out of two people suffer stress-related symptoms, and three out of four have stress on the job. We need to watch what we say. The word of God helps us overcome stress.

Here are eleven ways you can get rid of stress in your life.

1. Exercise regularly—this includes the spirit, soul, and body.

   "For bodily exercise has some value, but godliness has value in all things, having the promise of the life which is now, and of that which is to come. This saying is faithful and worthy of all acceptance. For to this end we both labor and suffer reproach, because we have set our trust in the living God, who is the Savior of all men, especially of those who believe. Command and teach these things."

   (1 Timothy 4:8–11 WEB)

2. We need to train our spirit so we don't tense up—tensing up causes too much adrenalin in our bodies. We need to crucify our body every day. In other words, don't let worldly things control your flesh. Take full control of your body and mind. Most of us let various stresses control us until they make us sick.

3. Anticipate stressful events and plan Godly solutions and think about bathing in prayer to make it through difficult times.

   "That no advantage may be gained over us by Satan; for we are not ignorant of his schemes."

   (2 Corinthians 2:11 WEB)

   Do not be ignorant of Satan's devices when it comes to your very existence.

   "You will show me the path of life. In your presence is fullness of joy. In your right hand there are pleasures forever more."

   (Psalm 16:11 WEB)

4. We need to talk over our personal problems with a friend, and His name is Jesus. Get on your prayer phone and call your Father God first in every situation.

   "Cast thy burden upon the Lord, and he shall sustain thee: he shall never suffer the righteous to be moved."
   (Psalm 55:22)

   He will never allow the righteous to be moved. Cast all your cares onto the Lord God, and He will never leave your side.

   "David was greatly distressed because the men were talking of stoning him; each one was bitter in spirit because of his sons and daughters. But David found strength in the Lord his God."
   (1 Samuel 30:6 KJV)

5. Get the clutter out of your house and out of your work space. It will reduce your stress.

   "The reason I left you in Crete was that you might put in order what was left unfinished and appoint elders in every town, as I directed you."
   (Titus 1:5 KJV)

   We need to set things in order in our lives.

6. Avoid verbal traps and line up your speech with what the Word says you can do. You can do all things in Christ who gives you the strength to do the impossible.

   *"You are trapped by the words of your mouth.
   You are ensnared with the words of your mouth."*
   (Proverbs 6:2 WEB)

"I tell you that every idle word that men speak, they will give account of it in the Day of Judgment. For by your words you will be justified, and by your words you will be condemned."
(Matthew 12:36–37 WEB)

Watch every idle word that comes out of your mouth.

*"He who guards his mouth guards his soul.
One who opens wide his lips come to ruin."*
(Proverbs 13:3 WEB)

By the word of my mouth I can set the tone of the day.

7. Put things in perspective. Keep the perspective that Jesus is coming soon.

8. No time to waste. Learn to accept and adapt to change.

"Therefore don't be anxious, saying, 'What will we eat?', 'What will we drink?' or, 'With what will we be clothed?' For the Gentiles seek after all these things; for your heavenly Father knows that you need all these things. But seek first God's Kingdom, and his righteousness; and all these things will be given to you as well. Therefore don't be anxious for tomorrow, for tomorrow will be anxious for itself. Each day's own evil is sufficient."
(Matthew 6:31 WEB)

9. Know your limits:

- Rest your body.

- Learn to say no to people.

- God can strengthen us and help us.

- Conviction keeps us in a balanced state.

- Condemnation is from the devil.

- Do what God tells you to do.

Can any one of you by worrying add a single hour to your life?

"And why do you worry about clothes? See how the flowers of the field grow. They do not labor or spin. Yet I tell you that not even Solomon in all his splendor was dressed like one of these. If that is how God clothes the grass of the field, which is here today and tomorrow is thrown into the fire, will he not much more clothe you—you of little faith? So do not worry, saying, 'What shall we eat?' or 'What shall we drink?' or 'What shall we wear?"

(Matthew 6:27–31 NIV)

When I was a young man living at home, my mother would just let every kind of worry come into her life. This sent her to the hospital on more than one occasion. Worry will not help solve your problems. Worrying about things will make a tough situation get worse.

This Scripture is just telling us to put our trust in God and go on with our lives. It is that simple: just meditate on good things like a few of these Scriptures that you've read throughout this book.

*Here is one of my favorite scriptures for worry."*Don't let your hearts be troubled. Trust in God, and trust also in me.

(John 14:1 NIV)

"For which I also labor, striving according to his working, which works in me mightily."

(Colossians 1:29 WEB)

God will energize me to do what God calls me to do.

"I can do all things through Christ, who strengthens me."

(Philippians 4:13 WEB)

This is a good one to remember.

10. Try cooperation instead of confrontation. Confrontation causes stress. Don't let minor aggravations bother you.

"A gentle answer turns away wrath,
  But a harsh word stirs up anger."

(Proverbs 15:1 WEB)

Come back with a soft word when someone comes at you with a confrontational attitude and see what happens.

"One who is slow to anger is better than the mighty;
One who rules his spirit, than he who takes a city."

(Proverbs 16:32 WEB)

I have a really bad temper and have to watch this daily. I don't want to submit to this part of my nature.

Whatever you do in life, remember this proverb.

"If the spirit of the ruler rises up against you, don't leave your place; for gentleness lays great offenses to rest."

(Ecclesiastes 10:4 WEB)

*"Pride only breeds quarrels,
But with ones who take advice is wisdom."*

(Proverbs 13:10 WEB)

Only by pride comes contention.

11. Make more time for fun and relaxation resting in the Lord.

"Redeeming the time, because the days are evil."

(Ephesians 5:16 WEB)

Make the most of your time each day and take time for yourself, which is very beneficial.

"Be still before the LORD and wait patiently for him; do not fret when people succeed in their ways, when they carry out their wicked schemes."

(Psalm 37:7 NIV)

Rest in the Lord so you can take on whatever the world throws at you.

"This is what the LORD says: "Stand at the crossroads and look; ask for the ancient paths, ask where the good way is, and walk in it, and you will find rest for your souls. But you said, 'We will not walk in it."

(Jeremiah 6:16 NIV)

Walk in the tried and true. Walk in faith.

"Come to me, all you who labor and are heavily burdened, and I will give you rest. Take my yoke upon you, and learn from me, for I am gentle and humble in heart; and you will find rest for your souls. For my yoke is easy, and my burden is light."

(Matthew 11:28 NIV)

There is a rest in God once we learn to trust Him.

Here are three ways to deal with stress quickly:

- Pray in the Holy Spirit

- Praise and worship God

- Take time each day to meditate on the Word

I have found out in life if I follow these instructions the stresses that come into my day will go away.

Chapter 43

My Near-Death Experience

"By Russell Morrison"

"My Father's house has many rooms;
   if that were not so, would I have told you that I am going there to
prepare a place for you."

—John 14:2 (NIV)

As a young child, I gave my life to Jesus, became a new believer in Christ and knew I wanted to follow him for the rest of my life. Then came my teenage years and I was led down a road of being cool and lost from where I came from. This road I was traveling down seemed to be very inviting, but it caused me to have major sadness, guilt and despair.

My mother and I moved from Oklahoma City and the dysfunctional family that I was born into. We moved to a small Arkansas town. My older sister moved in with a family that loved her as one of their own and provded for her a place to finish her childhood.

My hands are trembling a little as write this story due to an interesting conversation I had with my sister recently about a few things that happened to me over forty-two years ago. I had been working on finishing this book, and thought I had all of the chapters completed, but after talking to her, I decided to add this one.

My wife, who had been listening to the conversation with my sister, said she was getting goose bumps. My wife and I knew my side of the story but had never heard my sister's side of what happened to me as a teenager. I had called my sister the other night to see if she was feeling well, since my nephew let everyone know on social media that he and my sister had been sick for a week or so. When I called her, she hadn't answered, so I left a message.

Within a half hour or so, she called my wife, and they carried on a conversation about what was going in their parts of the world. My sister said that she was having a few health problems, had had a few tests done, and should know the results within a few days.

My wife and sister had a very good time on the phone, and then I had my chance to talk to her. We talked about our past and the things that had happened to both of us. We went back and forth from the past to the present in our conversation, talking about the good and bad things that we had lived through since we were both in different states than we were as teenagers.

I went on to tell her that I had a very close call with my heart and went into A-fib while I was at work. Thank God I work in one of the finest heart hospitals in the country. I was making my daily rounds throughout each department to make sure that the maintenance and housekeeping needs were up to par with what is expected of me in my role as a facilities director. I went up to the nurses' desk, told the staff that my heart was racing, and said that I might want to have them to check it out to see what was going on.

My Near-Death Experience

At that point, I was not stressed out or even concerned. I knew where I was, and I was in the best hands that you could be in. I knew that my personal health was going to be OK.

The team of doctors and outstanding nurses, along with the medication that brought my heart rate from 170 beats per minute to 120 within a short period of time, was working in my favor, but I was not out of the woods yet. The ER doctor must have contacted the cardiologist on call and had them start some medication to slow my heart down. Once the on-call doctor arrived, he noticed that my heart was still racing, gave the order to start another medication, and said he would be back in fifteen minutes to see if the new medication could bring my heart back into a normal rhythm.

After fifteen minutes or so, he came back and placed his stethoscope on my heart. Within seconds, my heart went back into the correct rhythm. At that time, I knew this physician had a special gift and that he really had the call to heal and comfort the sick. It seems that all the doctors here go out of their way to make sure they take care of their patients' physical healing, but they don't forget about tending to the spiritual man as well.

Within a short few hours, I was doing much better and was sent home. I told my sister that my test reports were good and that the doctors had placed me on a few more meds and told me that I would be fine.

My sister went on to say that she remembered our mom telling her another story about my heart stopping. She had found me unresponsive and had prayed and worked to bring me back to life. By the time she got started with her story about my mom saving me, my curiosity was about to go through the roof.

Juanita's Gift

She told me that when I was around sixteen or so, I came home and told her that I had been experimenting with things I should have not been doing. I also told her that my heart was racing and that I thought I might be in major trouble or could be having a heart attack. I didn't know my sister even knew anything about this story and don't remember telling her.

My sister went on to say that when I came home from a night of partying, I went into my very small bedroom and started pulling things off the walls. My sister went on to say that I landed on the floor, that I stopped breathing, and that my mom knew my heart had stopped beating. My mother had to hit me in the chest to get my heart beating more than once, and this occurred several times. I don't remember this part of my own story, but I remember a lot of other things that had happened to me. I told her I had no idea about this part of the story. She went on to say that Mom said I was on the floor, and as I became conscious again, I began to shout that I had seen Jesus.

So then I gave her my part of story. I was a very wild teenager and experimented with things that would just about end my life that night. I know now that my heart must have stopped, with my mother screaming to God to save me.

I'm fifty-eight years old now, and this story was so unexpected. As a teenager, I lived a year or so burning the candle around the middle and at both ends; I remember working eighty hours per week that summer to make a little extra money, but kept on going without sleep to party.

I told my sister that during that night forty-two years ago, I thought I had died. I went on to tell her that Ifelt like I was falling from one of the tallest mountains in Arkansas, and then I hit the bottom. Once I hit the bottom, I was in a very bright space. This space seemed to be very sterile, brilliant, with a bright light that totally encompassed what seemed like an endless space. I also noticed there were endless steps, like at the capitol building in Little Rock or any state capital; they were inconceivable in length and depth, went from left to right, and I could not see where they ended in any direction. I realized they were endless.

During this time, I cried out to Jesus to save me and bring me back. There was a supernatural being standing right in front of me, and I knew that it must have been Jesus. I know this must be one of the wildest stories you have ever heard, but it's really something that happened to me. I remember speaking to Him, and He spoke back to me. I remember a Bible verse said that says that when Jesus speaks, it's like a roaring river:

> "And his feet like unto fine brass, as if they burned in a furnace; and his voice as the sound of many waters."
> —Revelations 1:15 (NIV)

I also looked at Him while He spoke to me. I do not remember what He said, but it seemed that once He was done speaking, I was back in my house and was no longer under the influence of the many substances I put in my body that night.

I know without a doubt that God had a special reason for me to come back, to share my experiences with others, and to have children and live such an interesting life beyond anything that most can imagine. I'm not proud of how I lived back then, but I know in my heart that I was given a second chance to make a difference in my own life to help others. After that experience, I began to work diligently to help others pull themselves out of situations similar to the one that just about ended my life.

Juanita's Gift

I knew that I had to give something back, and I did so by helping seniors in nursing homes, young people, and those struggling with drugs. I shared about my faith and what happened to me to those in need in several area hospitals. For many years. It was an experience that changed my life. From then on, I quit the partying and tried to live as God wanted me to.

It had been years since I had told this story. I have been writing this book for a year or so and didn't even think about putting this story in the book until I spoke with my sister on the phone.

The conversation with my sister really took me back to what happened that night. I knew that I most likely died or had a near-death experience, but I had not heard the story about what my mother went through while watching me. All I know is that my mother loved me and prayed to God to save me. I'm astounded to think that I didn't know the entire story about my loving mother who brought me into this world but didn't want me to leave it that way.

I have been so blessed to have had her there to pray for me. My sister said she prayed and kept watch until I was OK. What a shocking part of the story that I didn't even know about! It reminds me that God gave me a second chance at having a wonderful life, and I certainly have had that life.

Story by Becky Parker

Son died -God restored alive to his mother

It has been close to 42 years now that my Mother told me a story of horror about my brother who she said died and God restored alive to her.

My Near-Death Experience

I remember her in tears as she recounted how my brother had stopped breathing and turned blue one night. She realized he'd overdosed on something but had no idea on what. He told her his heart was racing so fast that he felt like he was having a heart attack.

She said: He was scaring her so bad. He was talking out of his head about Jesus and passed out. She said" "I leaned down to listen to him breathe. Put my head on his chest to hear his heart. Nothing! He was dying or was already dead? I began screaming at him. Wake up! Now! Wake up! Don't you die on me!" She began beating his chest with her fist trying to restart his heart. Again, she listened and nothing. He was turning blue and not responding. It was then she knew she was going to lose him. He was gone. She cried out to Jesus. "God, please hear me. Save my baby! Help me Jesus. Don't take him please…" She said; "Then all of a sudden!" she heard him say; "Mom?" He began to tell her about something he saw while he was unconscious. He told her how he thought he had seen Jesus.

Mom told me she knew God spared my little brother's life that night for something and she was so happy He did!

Chapter 44

Building the Temple

"For through him we both have our access in one Spirit to the Father. So then you are no longer strangers and foreigners, but you are fellow citizens with the saints, and of the household of God, being built on the foundation of the apostles and prophets, Christ Jesus himself being the chief cornerstone; in whom the whole building, fitted together, grows into a holy temple in the Lord; in whom you also are built together for a habitation of God in the Spirit."

(Ephesians 2:19–21 WEB)

Make Jesus our cornerstone so we have a strong foundation to our faith. Laying the foundation of our faith is the key component to our children's success along with being responsible at the same time to instruct our children in the ways of the Lord. A strong foundation under them will enable them to survive the storms of life. A weak foundation will weaken the entire spiritual structure. Without a strong foundation the temple will fall.

Temptation to hurry up and think you are finished growing in the Spirit could cause you to fall. To grow as Christians we need to start out with the milk of the Word and go from baby food to bite-size table food and then to meat.

Meat of the Word is the agape love of God. The hardest food to chew and the hardest to swallow often causes us to choke on the more complicated parts of God's Word.

A mature Christian is the one who is walking in the love of God and has been made alive in Christ and has been delivered from the things that are trying to control his flesh.

> *"You were made alive when you were dead in transgressions and sins, in which you once walked according to the course of this world, according to the prince of the power of the air, the spirit who now works in the children of disobedience; among whom we also all once lived in the lust of our flesh, doing the desires of the flesh and of the mind, and were by nature children of wrath, even as the rest. But God, being rich in mercy, for his great love with which he loved us, even when we were dead through our trespasses, made us alive together with Christ (by grace you have been saved), and raised us up with him, and made us to sit with him in the heavenly places in Christ Jesus, that in the ages to come he might show the exceeding riches of his grace in kindness toward us in Christ Jesus; for by grace you have been saved through faith, and that not of yourselves; it is the gift of God, not of works, that no one would boast. For we are his workmanship, created in Christ Jesus for good works, which God prepared before that we would walk in them."*
>
> (Ephesians 2:1–10 WEB)

By becoming a believer in Christ your spirit becomes alive in Christ, and your foundation that supports your Christian walk will not fail you. The foundation we need to lay is Jesus Christ. Avoid cracks in your spiritual foundation to prevent it from collapsing.

Don't let anything slow your Christian growth down or the special walk that you have started with God. We must do a thorough job on the spiritual foundation that supports everything that we are and we can continue to become Christ like in who we are.

Chapter 45

Life and Power of Words

Faith causes the Word to live in you.

I have to release faith in God's Words that I speak.

Watch what you say about others and don't try to bring them down or destroy them with words. Only say and think in the positive about those people that have hurt you. Forgive those that lie about you and your family. I have noticed in so many cases that people can say a lot of bad things about you or even your business and most of the time people will believe those lies. People like to cause dissention, to control, or steal from others by causing them to look unlikable. When you are talking about someone, only use words that are positive, or don't say anything at all.

> "For the word of God is living and active, and sharper than any two-edged sword, piercing even to the dividing of soul and spirit, of both joints and marrow, and is able to discern the thoughts and intentions of the heart."
>
> (Hebrew 4:12)

God's Word is more powerful than those negative words that come against us. Faith is the divine energy of God's Word. God's Word is His will. Words that are not His will are idle words. We need to take God's Word and speak it and believe it.

God's Word first has to be in my mouth then in my heart. One of the first things you need to do is speak God's Word until your faith comes. Speak God's Word daily and you will see the evidence appear in how your faith will grow.

Faith comes by hearing God's Word.

I add life when I speak God's Word. Getting rid of doubt is a process by getting our minds renewed with the Word of God.

God's Word is alive when I read it and speak it, and it will be manifested in my life.

People are often limited in their speech, and they speak as the world speaks.

I plant seeds, good or bad seeds, by the words that I speak.

You can plant good seeds of faith and you will produce fruit that will last you a life time. You can plant seeds that don't produce fruit and they will be like weeds in your personal garden that will choke out the things that are going to make you prosper in your daily walk.

My wife, Patti, and I were discussing the summer heat and how the flower beds were still looking good. She told me she had a funny story about a certain plant. One of the men in the area, who is always trying to make a little money, seems to come by once a week to help us pull a few weeds.

Life and Power of Words

My wife asked him to get started in the back part of the flower bed and went on pulling weeds in her section of the flower beds. After working for a while, my wife noticed how he had been cultivating this very tall plant. My wife came a little closer to the flower bed that he was working in so she could see just what he had been spending his time on throughout the summer. It was a very large and beautiful green weed, but because it was a weed, it had never flowered and borne fruit. He seemed pretty proud that he had kept such a large weed alive and that it was still thriving in our lovely Arkansas summer heat.

A lady who was walking by, took in the conversation, smiled, and walked on by. The lady was most likely thinking, "Good luck with teaching a man which things to pull out of the flower bed." On many occasions, I have pulled the flowers out instead of the weeds. I do love flowers and am fairly knowledgeable, but I still want to learn more each season.

I think many times in our lives, we seem to cultivate the wrong things—those that don't really mean anything to us or even help us grow as a person. I have to examine myself routinely to be aware of what I'm thinking about or what is taking up my time daily. I want to stay prayed up and walk in the Spirit, and I don't want anything to enter into my mind that will interfere with that walk with God.

All authority is given by words.

Do you remember how many times in your life that you said, "I'm going to work hard so I can purchase that house or car?" "I'm going to be an engineer, cardiologist, or teacher" and later in life that is what you become.

Keep saying what you want and need and what you want to be in life. You believed in your own words. So why can't we believe in God's Words?

We can be successful in Christ and walk as he walked. Just keep the faith and continue to run the faith race so you will be able to claim your reward.

"Jerry Sprout's Story"

One person who inspired me in the last few months to keep a positive attitude about life was Jerry Sprout.

Jerry Sprout came into my office a year ago to let me know how much he liked the first book that I had written, "Juanita's Walk with God". His wife Peggy worked with me, and he wanted to congratulate me on writing my first book.

Jerry's doctor told him that he had kidney cancer and that there was nothing that he could do but wait to die. It really touched me that his wife was reading my book and sharing it with him. If my book touches or helps even one person to grow in their faith, it has accomplished what Juanita and I wanted it to and that was to point as many people toward heaven as we could. I feel Juanita is still sharing the gospel to the world through these books.

What a wonderful surprise to see Jerry and Peggy walking in the hallway of the hospital one day several months later. It was great to see Jerry out and about. What a miracle. He was walking with a cane and said he was doing fine, but I could tell he was having major pain in his leg. The cancer most likely has traveled to other parts of his body. I noticed him taking a pill at the water fountain for the pain.

Watching him I could tell that the pain was pretty bad. Fighting the cancer was really taking a toll on him. He told me that Peggy had still been reading him "the book" and that they were almost done with it. I told him I was writing another book and he responded by saying, "Hey, Russell, I'm almost done with the first book, and it has been very uplifting and inspirational, so hurry up with the second book!" Wow! That made my day and has caused me to write in overdrive to get it done.

That first book is working on a man that really needed it to help carry him all the way home to be with his heavenly Father. You know, if one book, one encouraging word to someone, or one little word of hope can really mean the world to someone like Jerry, it has been worth everything to me. We really need to take time to share our words of faith and love with those that we come in contact with each and every day. It will change your life and theirs. I have been so blessed by sharing my mother-in-law's faith and studying the inspiring notes she left behind.

I now realize how Christianity started by just a few people sharing the amazing life of Jesus. They could not stop telling people about someone who had changed their life. That's what has happened to me. I can't stop telling people how Jesus used people like Juanita to help change my life. I will never stop telling these stories.

Patti Morrison

Russell and I have a friend who is a great woman of faith. She has always lived her life according to God's Word. She raised four daughters who are also women of faith. Widowed at a relatively young age, Michelle continued to live a faith-based life. God provided for her and her family. Her children are educated and brilliant women. Recently Michelle has had some trials. In her late eighties, she had fallen and broken an ankle. Because of the broken ankle, she has had to spend some time in a rehab nursing home. Many people would be down and depressed, but Michelle has continually witnessed to the staff and residents. Recently a staff member who had made a few comments and laughed about Michelle's "being a Christian" later got her aside and asked if she would pray for their family, which shows what a witness her faith has been. How many of us could still keep our faith when facing circumstances such as being in a nursing home, locked away from our own home and things?

God takes care of us wherever we are and by His grace we are survivors and we should realize that this world is not our home but we are just passing through.

Chapter 46

Renewing Your Mind

"Therefore I urge you, brothers, by the mercies of God, to present your bodies a living sacrifice, holy, acceptable to God, which is your spiritual service. ² Don't be conformed to this world, but be transformed by the renewing of your mind, so that you may prove what is the good, well-pleasing, and perfect will of God."

(Romans 12: 1–2 WEB)

God is concerned about everything we do and wants to take part in our daily lives. My faith can change my outer situations. We all need to be teachable so it will be possible for God to mold us into His image and not the world's image. We need to make ourselves available to learn the lessons that come into our daily life each day. If not, you will not grow.

When these lessons of faith come, they are not always those lessons that will hurt your walk but will help you to grow as a more mature Christian.

I fight the negative thoughts that come in to try to control me and take complete control of who I am and all I want to do is run those negative things in my mind until they take my joy.

We have to hit the refresh button on our minds and start thinking on only the things that will bring us peace.

Doing this will transform our spirits and will renew our minds.

> "This I say therefore, and testify in the Lord, that you no longer walk as the rest of the Gentiles also walk, in the futility of their mind, being darkened in their understanding, alienated from the life of God, because of the ignorance that is in them, because of the hardening of their hearts; who having become callous gave themselves up to lust, to work all uncleanness with greediness. But you did not learn Christ that way; if indeed you heard him, and were taught in him, even as truth is in Jesus: that you put away, as concerning your former way of life, the old man, that grows corrupt after the lusts of deceit; and that you be renewed in the spirit of your mind, and put on the new man, who in the likeness of God has been created in righteousness and holiness of truth."
>
> "Therefore putting away falsehood speak truth each one with his neighbor. For we are members of one another. "Be angry, and don't sin." Don't let the sun go down on your wrath, and don't give place to the devil. Let him who stole steal no more; but rather let him labor, producing with his hands something that is good, that he may have something to give to him who has need. Let no corrupt speech proceed out of your mouth, but only what is good for building others up as the need may be, that it may give grace to those who hear. Don't grieve the Holy Spirit of God, in whom you were sealed for the day of redemption. Let all bitterness, wrath, anger, outcry, and slander, be put away from you, with all malice. And be kind to one another, tender hearted, forgiving each other, just as God also in Christ forgave you."
>
> (Ephesians 4:17–23 WEB)

You can access it by faith, placing all your thoughts on Him, keeping your mind in complete submission so you can walk right into the grace of God. Grace will empower me to do all things I otherwise couldn't do. For instance, Russell, you can write a book. This is book number two, and both are miracles. Again, I think I'm getting a little help from Juanita who resides in heaven giving me a push or one big shove. Juanita was one of my many mentors who kept pushing me and helping me believe in myself and saying all the way, "You can do all things in Christ who strengthens you." Keep your mind focused on Him.

> "Jesus said to him, "You shall love the Lord your God with all your heart, with all your soul, and with all your mind."
>
> (Matthew 22:37 KJV)

We are to carry such an influence to others that others know that God is in their presence. Am I standing by faith? Am I growing in grace? We must value what Jesus valued and influence others as Jesus did by being in complete control of our minds. The mind of Christ will take me all the way to be more like Him.

Faith, grace, favor, and glory were all terms noted by Juanita and she listened for His voice daily so she could grow in His grace and favor. Slow down each day to meditate on His thoughts. One thing I go back to when I think of changing my thought pattern is the fruits of the spirit. If you are thinking these thoughts, you're on the right track.

Jesus opened the door for all of us to have fellowship with God. It's hard to believe that someone gave His life for a guy like me, but He did.

I'm so excited that I have another chance to get it right and all I have to do is surrender this old worldly flesh that enjoys being so sinful. His Word says it all, and it's by faith and not by sight that we can trust that He will take us in as one of His own.

"Set your mind on the things that are above, not on the things that are on the earth."

(Colossians 3:2 WEB)

"Finally, brothers, whatever things are true, whatever things are honorable, whatever things are just, whatever things are pure, whatever things are lovely, whatever things are of good report; if there is any virtue, and if there is any praise, think about these things."

(Philippians 4:8 WEB)

Chapter 47

Spiritual Authority

What gives us the authority over the earth we live in?

> *"Having been born again, not of corruptible seed, but of incorruptible, through the word of God, which lives and remains forever."*
> (1 Peter 1:23 WEB)

I'm born again of incorruptible seed. Faith as a seed will grow into something very special. The world is filled with many types of seeds. Which kind are you?

I'm a good seed. Corruptible seed is the seed of man. I'm here for a purpose, and I'm an incorruptible seed of God. I'm born again of an incorruptible seed.

My heavily Father has delegated authority to me. I'm born again of an incorruptible seed.

My heavenly Father has delegated authority to me. I'm His child.

"But as many as received him, to them he gave the right to become God's children, to those who believe in his name.

(John 1:12 WEB)

He called to himself his twelve disciples, and gave them authority over unclean spirits, to cast them out, and to heal every disease and every sickness.

(Matthew 10:1 WEB)

Anointing comes when we take authority. How much authority do we have?

"Having the eyes of your hearts enlightened, that you may know what is the hope of his calling, and what are the riches of the glory of his inheritance in the saints."

(Ephesians 1:16–18 ESV)

How much revelation I have of the Word of God is how much authority I have. I now am fully understanding in the vision of our hearts, I'm His body.

Being in His fullness means we are a full container. I'm a container of life, and that life is the glory and honor of God. As vessels of His Holy Spirit, we contain God's Spirit in us. *Thinking about these few words really made me think about how much power we all can possess by just trusting God.*

I do have authority over the devil, Juanita wrote.

"This is how love is made complete among us so that we will have confidence on the day of judgment: In this world we are like Jesus."

(1 John 4:17 NIV)

Do we have the right to pray against principalities and powers? Yes we do!

> *"He who sins is of the devil, for the devil has been sinning from the beginning. To this end the Son of God was revealed: that he might destroy the works of the devil."*
>
> (1 John 3:8 WEB)

Jesus' purpose was to destroy the works of the devil and to give us life. Jesus came to put the devil out of business and He did. I am here to put the devil out of business. We are to exterminate the works of the devil. But we are no threat to the devil when we are so consumed with meeting our needs.

> *"I will give you thanks with my whole heart."*
>
> (Psalm 138:1 WEB)

We must have the right attitude toward God. We are here with a purpose, and that is to praise God and to serve Him.

> *"Finally, be strong in the Lord, and in the strength of his might. Put on the whole armor of God that you may be able to stand against the wiles of the devil. For our wrestling is not against flesh and blood, but against the principalities, against the powers, against the world's rulers of the darkness of this age, and against the spiritual forces of wickedness in the heavenly places. Therefore put on the whole armor of God that you may be able to withstand in the evil day, and, having done all, to stand."*
>
> (Ephesians 6:10–14 WEB)

Christians are to be prayed up at all times so you can withstand the principalities and the chief of principalities. Pray in God's Spirit to disrupt the evil that we see each day.

We fight against evil spirits, and they are against us and want to destroy every part of our lives. Evil spirits want to take as many souls to hell as they can, and they don't want Christians slowing down the agenda they have for the human race.

The only way the devil can get into our spirit is if we let him in. Whatever you feed your spirit will open doors for a lot of unfriendly things to come in.

We can exercise our authority by prayer and intercession, speaking the Word of God, and then doing the works of Jesus.

> "Men fainting for fear, and for expectation of the things which are coming on the world: for the powers of the heavens will be shaken."
>
> (Luke 21:26 WEB)

Stay prayed up at all times so you can run this race for your very soul. Don't give up when the storms of life come against you or when you get a bad report. Remember—trust in Him, and don't let your hearts be troubled.

Chapter 48

A Rock in the Caribbean

"By Raymond Whitten"

Don Francisco wrote a song about the story of Jesus raising Jairius's daughter from the dead. As the story goes, after He had raised the little girl back to life, he admonished everyone to see to it that they told no one. In the song, written from the perspective of the father of the little girl, Jairius could not help himself. He just had to "tell somebody what Jesus did for me." This is how I feel right now.

I have struggled with the telling of this story, not in the sense that I hesitate to tell it, but in the sense that I haven't had the venue to tell it enough. It is a story that I wish everyone could hear or read. It is true. And, it happened to me. And I cry almost every time I think about it.

We were on vacation. This was a special vacation, the first time my wife and I had been out of the country together. We were celebrating several things, like the marriage of our daughter the week before, the fact that we were now "empty nesters," our twenty-nine years together as husband and wife, and my fifty-fifth birthday. We actually flew out on my birthday to St. Martin where we spent the next week.

Harriet, my wife, is probably one of the most practical-minded individuals I have ever met. While we were in St. Martin, to help offset some of the expense, and to be able to do some special things, she set us up to tour some time-share condominiums. As it turned out, our friends with whom we were vacationing actually bought a week in St. Martin. But, more to the point, one of the things we "won" was a snorkeling trip out to a desert island called Prickly Pear. Now, keep in mind, by the time we took this snorkeling trip, we had already been on St. Martin for four days. We had a wonderful vacation, and we didn't even play any golf! I had to get a shot of prednisone for my sun allergy, and Harriet was deathly ill for one whole day, but other than that, we just enjoyed the blessing of God and resorted, played, relaxed, visited, saw the sights, toured time-shares, and over all just had fun. And then we sailed out to Prickly Pear.

This was a really top-drawer sailing/snorkeling trip. We sailed for almost two hours out into the Caribbean and dropped anchor out in the bay, about a couple of hundred yards from the shore. The crew handed out the snorkeling gear, really nice full-foot flippers and masks, and instructed everyone to get into the water and snorkel for however long and make it to the beach in about an hour for lunch. Harriet and I went off the back of the boat, with her going first. When I got into the water and put my head under, I realized that my beard and mustache wouldn't allow my mask to seal properly and water was continually seeping into my mask. I was fussing with this, snorting out the water from my mask as I tried to see under water and take some pictures with the little disposable camera I had bought before leaving the dock in St. Martin. All the while, I was flippering away from the boat so as to not be in anyone else's way, and also to try to keep up with Harriet who is not a very strong swimmer and was having trouble just staying afloat. In not too long, I started feeling my chest tighten and I thought to myself that

A Rock in the Caribbean

I was probably hyperventilating, something I tend to do when I exert myself. So, I tried to slow down, even floating on my back for a while. I told Harriet that we should probably go on to the beach because I was having a little trouble, but then, when I looked for the beach, I saw that we had swam past the sandy part of the beach, and the nearest shore was what appeared to be rocks. By now, I didn't care whether I made shore on rocks or sand, because my chest was really hurting. I couldn't seem to get my "hyperventilating" under control. I was getting a little panicked and told Harriet "I'm in trouble." I have to admit that it occurred to me that I might be having some heart problems, but since I had had no pain before in times of much more strenuous exertion, I discounted it almost immediately. But, I knew that hyperventilating can be just as serious, especially in the ocean where you can't just stop and rest and catch your breath. I honestly was afraid of drowning. I finally shouted, as best I could, to Harriet to send the little inflatable dingy after me when she made it to shore. She has described to me how helpless she felt at that time. I hate even thinking how frightening that was to her.

Remember those rocks I was headed for? Well, by now I was close enough to see that they weren't rocks at all, but were a coral reef. I had no idea what kind they were, but they were shaped like serrated knife blades pointing in every different direction, with points several inches long. I tried to swim away from them, but by now I had no strength in my legs and no air in my lungs. I was completely at the mercy of the ocean waves that were taking me directly to the coral. I kept getting closer and closer, and as I did, I realized that I was about to be dashed to pieces on them before I had a chance to drown. I knew, I say <u>knew</u>, that I was about to die.

I was no farther than ten feet away from the coral. I was still trying to flipper away, very feebly by now, and felt through the flippers the sharp edges of the coral beneath me. I have failed to mention that there had been two hurricanes that passed to the North and to the South the day before, and the waves were fairly nasty as a result. Weird as I am, I had timed the waves and estimated that within the next three waves, I would be washed upon these incredibly sharp, deadly coral and would then be moved with the ocean and cut to shreds. It would be slow, ugly, painful, and ultimately fatal. And it was inevitable. I can't begin to express the degree of certainty about this. I was angry and confused because I have this sense of being special to God, and although I know I have disappointed Him on numerous occasions, I also knew and know that there are still things that He has for me to do. I couldn't understand how this could be. But ultimately, I was terrified. There was no more presumption in me. This was not one that He was going to just nonchalant me out of. I was at the end. So, I cried out with my voice. I didn't have time for a fancy prayer. If I had started when my chest had started hurting, maybe I would have had time, but I didn't. There's a lesson there. What I did do was to cry out for what I thought I needed. I cried "Lord, give me a rock to stand on."

This is where I begin to cry.

<u>Immediately</u> after I cried out, my little worn-out bottom washed up on a smooth, flat rock. Right in the middle of all that coral. But I was still not out of trouble. Those of you who have been in the ocean know that the ocean does what the ocean is going to do, and if you are in it, you will do it with the ocean. And, the ocean was still trying to wash me into shore onto the coral. I realized that I would have to grab something and hold on, but also knew that I would likely cut my hand to shreds grabbing. But I knew I had to stay on that rock, so I reached out my left hand, and grabbed. I don't know how to describe what I grabbed except to call it a handhold. It was on the side of the rock I was sitting on and it was as if

it had been shaped for my hand. It even had a place for my thumb and was just the right size. I knew then that I would be able to hold on, but the waves were still crashing in on me and holding on with one hand was not ideal. By now, also, I had figured out that God had answered my cry, so I reasoned that if there was a handhold on one side, there might be one on the other side. So, I gingerly reached out with my right hand, and what do you think I found? That's right, another handhold, just like the one on the other side, with a place for my thumb.

Now remember, I was in pain and out of breath and strength. So, I just sat there, holding onto my rock, until the pain subsided and I got my breath and strength back. Harriet had made it to shore and dispatched the little dingy out for me, but they said that I couldn't hold onto them or we would both wash up on the coral. They instructed me to get on my back and swim on to the sandy beach. By then I had gotten my strength back and was able to do just that. I was strong enough to push away from the coral and flipper to the shore. By the time I got to shore my chest was hurting again and I was an emotional wreck. By this time, our friends had come to shore to find us (They'd gone off the front of the boat and lost track of us.) and they and Harriet helped me to one of the picnic benches to lie down. One of our friends is an RN and assessed that I had experienced a heart attack. There is no 911 in the middle of the ocean or she would have called it. For my part, I was just embarrassed because I had slipped into denial and was maintaining that I had just hyperventilated.

As we were flying back to the states, Harriet shared the story with our friends from her perspective, which included her panic when she realized that I was in serious trouble. She told of the spiritual warfare that went on with Satan telling her that he was going to kill me in front of her and there wasn't a thing she could do about it. I was still very much in denial about what had actually been going on, but she, being much more sensitive spiritually than I at the time, knew in her heart what had happened. She maintained all the time that I had to have been having a heart attack. I simply refused to consider it. After all, I didn't have any more pain. Well, maybe just a little. I think I knew, but I just was not prepared to accept all that that would mean. Anyway, when a month later my boss threatened to fire me if I didn't have a physical, I went.

My doctor looked and listened and said I sounded okay. He ran an EKG and it looked normal, but to be thorough, especially after hearing that I'd experienced chest pains a month earlier, he scheduled a stress test for the next day. I lasted less than four minutes before I was having "really uncomfortable" chest pains and he stopped the test. The EKG still looked normal to him, but he recommended that I have a heart catheterization done. At first, I tried to reason my way out of that, but he said, "Ray, God doesn't give us too many warnings, and when he does, we need to listen." Those were just the right words to say, I guess, because I agreed to the procedure. The next morning, after being assured by the cardiologist that he didn't expect to find much based on my exams so far, we found out that I had one artery completely blocked, one 98% blocked, and another 99% blocked. I had triple bypass surgery the next morning.

Not only had God provided a miracle in the form of a rock in the middle of the Caribbean, he had been keeping me alive for only He knows how long with only a trickle of blood to my heart.

I have learned so much from this. I have learned to appreciate the everyday blessings we so easily take for granted. I have always known my wife loves me, but I know more now how deep and sacrificing that love is. I am familiar with pain much more intimately now, the kind that is associated with death. This makes me so much more appreciative of the sacrifice Jesus made for me. He didn't have a morphine drip. He knew how great the pain would be when he willingly went to Calvary's Cross. But He still went.

Chapter 49

Renew Our Relationship

Juanita noted in one of her journals that women need to establish trust with friends and develop good relationships that last. She wrote down the words of a speaker she had heard: "I'm an amazing woman." She most likely was. She was also very confident in who she was and what she was doing with her life.

God gives us grace to get done the things we need to do.

Thank God for the women in my life who have pushed and pulled me to get off my backside—so that I could get a few things accomplished in this life! Most of us men need those confident, strong women who are amazing and who motivate us into a better walk with God and most of the time a better life.

Even today I can imagine my mother-in-law is still pushing me to write these books and share the gospel. Sounds crazy, but that's how I feel. I feel that she is pushing me all the way from heaven to get it done. Thanks for the push of confidence, Juanita! Just like a mother-in-law to just keep pushing and praying that this project gets completed. I can imagine my daughter is right next to her forcefully doing the same to get this book published so I can start sharing it with others.

"But on the first day of the week, at early dawn, they and some others came to the tomb, bringing the spices which they had prepared. They found the stone rolled away from the tomb. They entered in, and didn't find the Lord Jesus' body While they were greatly perplexed about this, behold, two men stood by them in dazzling clothing Becoming terrified, they bowed their faces down to the earth."

"They said to them, "Why do you seek the living among the dead? He isn't here, but is raised. Remember what he told you when he was still in Galilee, saying that the Son of Man must be delivered up into the hands of sinful men, and be crucified, and the third day rise again?"

"They remembered his words, returned from the tomb, and told all these things to the eleven, and to all the rest. Now they were Mary Magdalene, Joanna, and Mary the mother of James. The other women with them told these things to the apostles. These words seemed to them to be nonsense, and they didn't believe them. But Peter got up and ran to the tomb. Stooping and looking in, he saw the strips of linen lying by themselves, and he departed to his home, wondering what had happened."

(Luke 24:1–12 WEB)

A woman in the gospel of Luke found that Jesus was missing from the tomb after the crucifixion and told the men that He was missing. This motivated woman was one of many women of God that most likely got the ball rolling to jump-start Christianity. I would say that women of faith are still one of the motivating factors that most men need to get them going in the right direction into the light of Christ.

This news of the resurrection amazed the men, and the story of Jesus' missing body must have sent a shockwave through their own hearts.

What a great day this has been working on my book and reading this Scripture on the day before Easter. This to me was another divine appointment.

"But the Advocate, the Holy Spirit, whom the Father will send in my name, will teach you all things and will remind you of everything I have said to you. Peace I leave with you; my peace I give you. I do not give to you as the world gives. Do not let your hearts be troubled and do not be afraid."

"You heard me say, 'I am going away and I am coming back to you.' If you loved me, you would be glad that I am going to the Father, for the Father is greater than I. I have told you now before it happen, so that when it does happen you will believe. I will not say much more to you, for the prince of this world is coming. He has no hold over me."

(John 14:26 NIV)

The Holy Spirit brings to my remembrance of the Word that I need. Jesus is alive. We need to rise up and relax. I am an amazing woman, and I have an amazing message to share.

She did share her wonderful faith daily with everyone that she came in contact and challenged us to be more knowledgeable in Christ.

"Further, because the Preacher was wise, he still taught the people knowledge. Yes, he pondered, sought out, and set in order many proverbs. The Preacher sought to find out acceptable words, and that which was written blamelessly, words of truth. The words of the wise are like goods, increase, or develop and like nails well fastened are words from the masters of assemblies, which are given from one shepherd. Furthermore, my son be admonished: of making many books there is no end; and much study is a weariness of the flesh."

"This is the end of the matter. All has been heard. Fear God, and keep his commandments; for this is the whole duty of man. For God will bring every work into judgment, with every hidden thing, whether it is good, or whether it is evil."

(Ecclesiastes 12:9–13 WEB)

Chapter 50

Children Who Pray

"Story" by Russell Morrison

When a mother takes time to give a child instruction about prayer, she has done her job as a mother. I was very fortunate that my mother took me and my sister to a small church in Oklahoma City where the values of prayer were planted deep within who we were.

As a very young child, I can remember praying that God would help me with any type of situation or concerns that I had. I understood that prayer was just an open communication with our maker. We were taught that He was willing and ready to listen at any given time, and all I had to do is open up and let Him know what was going on in my small world.

My wife and I both tried to instill the same values in our children by planting a few ideas along the way, knowing that it would be very helpful to our children to have the same open communication. One thing I'm very proud of is that my granddaughters have been taught by their mother to pray daily. These girls pray over their meals and whatever comes up during the day.

Just the other day, my wife was having health problems, and my oldest granddaughter said. "Grandma, I know what will make you feel better." She went on to say, "Let me pray for you." She is twelve years old and an old soul who is very aware that we are more than just flesh and blood.

I was putting the last chapter in my book and asked both girls if they wanted to contribute something. The youngest girl, Lillian, said that her concern was about the poor in the world, and she wanted to be able to see what they were going through so she could pray for them. My other granddaughter said that she remembered the time her cousins were at their house, and a young boy was visiting from Pennsylvania. He was hurt very badly from a bicycle wreck, and one of the first things they did was pray.

A Mother's Prayers

I have been so amazed at the dedication of my daughter-in-law, Anna, in teaching all her children to pray. Even three-year-old James has been brought into the mix. She has worked diligently in teaching her young children the importance of prayer.

Written by Charlee M. Morrison, age twelve

My cousin came over to my house and brought her friend, who was named Adasen. That night, we had a big party for the whole neighborhood. Darian and Adasen were having a bike race. Adasen swerved and hit the ditch that was covered in rocks. He cut his face really badly, and his braces were ripped off of his teeth. Lillian was the first one to reach him. My dad, my aunt, and my uncle wrapped his face up with a towel and took him to the local ER. They said that we would have to take him to children's hospital because it was so bad. My cousins and my younger sister could not go, so we stayed home and prayed for him while listening to Christian music until one in the morining The next day, we heard from our parents that Adasen had to have surgery. By going to the children's hospital, he had gotten one of the best surgeons in the country, even though Adasen was from Pennsylvania and we are in Little Rock. We knew that our prayers had been answered because his face healed so well that you could hardly see a scar.

> *"All your children will be taught by the Lord, and great will be their peace."*
> —Isaiah 54:13 (NIV)

> *"Fathers, do not provoke your children, lest they become discouraged."*
> —Colossians 3:21 (NIV)

> *"Jesus said, 'Let the little children come to me, and do not hinder them, for the kingdom of heaven belongs to such as these.'"*
> —Mathew 19:14 (NIV)

Lillian's Prayer
Written by Lillian Morrison, age eleven

As a young child, I wonder if all people in the world are protected by God. I know I am. I know He is protecting all of us. Most people don't even know who God is. I think people have not been taught about prayer and God. I just want people to know God like I do.

I don't always know when someone is in need or hurting; even random people who walk by me might need my prayer. I pray that God gives me the eyes to see those who are in need. I will take time to say a prayer for them. Even if you're a little kid like me, you still want to be in tune to know what people's needs are. So many times, I feel in my spirit that those people are hurting, and I know they need a reason to believe in God.

I want to be like my mother, who taught me to pray and be good at praying for others, so I can help others grow. It makes me so sad to see the poor in the world. I really want to help them. It hurts to see those in need, and I know that with God things work out.

Where did these ideas of prayer come from? I can say that my daughter-in-law was taught by her mother and dad, and I personally know that my daughter-in-law's mother was taught by her mother.

> *"And my God shall supply every need of yours according to his riches in glory in Christ Jesus."*
>
> Philippians 4:19 (NIV)

God deals with us every day as we walk through this life. This is true in regard to food, clothing, shelter, and transportation.

I have a friend who has a child with Down syndrome; she also has five other children, so she has had to trust God to take care of their needs because it can get overwhelming. My wife makes slipcovers and drapes, and this friend is an excellent seamstress and has worked for my wife. On one of my wife's sewing jobs around 2013, my wife grabbed a pamphlet that was at the jobsite and wrote some measurements on it. She stuck it in her purse, used the measurements, and forgot about it. It must have gone in a pile of receipts because when she was doing her taxes, it reappeared on the kitchen island.

My wife, thinking it must belong to our friend because it was about children, gave it to her. Our friend called the number on the pamphlet, and now that organization is providing her with free diapers for her youngest child. This is just one example of how God takes care of our simplest of needs.

My hope and prayer is that mothers keep teaching their children about prayer and that they can have an open communication with the heavenly Father who will help them through this life and provide them with a spiritual home.

My mother-in-law noted in one of her journals that "the devil will not rob me of Charlee and Dudley." Charlee was fighting leukemia at the time of this prayer and was at Arkansas Children's Hospital struggling just to live another day; my father-in-law, her husband, Dudley, was fighting heart disease. My daughter lived eight more years after this prayer, and I do think that each and every day that my mother-in-law stayed on her knees before God, our prayers and hers were answered for the next eight years. Juanita is in His presence and is most likely praying for all of us here on earth who struggle each and every day with finding our way.

I hope you enjoyed all of Juanita's journal notes, plus a few stories of faith, struggles, and hope.

Putting her journals into these chapters has been one incredible ride that I will never forget.

Reading her journals each and every day really made me think about my own personal walk. I know now how one can improve his or her own personal faith walk by taking a few minutes each day to meditate, pray, and read His Word.

Once I began doing this, it caused me to change for the better. I know putting this book together came about because of one source. I had never thought about writing a book until I read her wonderful journals, and that's how it all began. I don't claim to be a writer. I think the books are very raw and from the heart. I know it has touched my life, and maybe they were meant just for me. If so, I thank God they were given to me because they have changed my life. I pray that the book spoke to your heart as it did mine.

Made in the USA
San Bernardino, CA
16 December 2014